HOW TO TALK TO YOUR MUSLIM CHILD ABOUT SEX

Firoza Osman
Book design by: Rabia Akter

Introduction..3

Chapter 1..13
The Challenge of Raising Children in a Digital World

- Pick your battles/cultural norms/peer orientation
- Sex-obsessed Culture (sexualization of children; sexualization through music and music videos; sexualization in TV and movies; profanity)
- Gender-specific Issues – Girls; Boys (desensitization caused by gaming; pornography)
- The Dangers of Social Media
- The School Environment– peer pressure and challenges; mental health challenges
- Dangers of Drugs
- Alcohol
- Muslim-Specific Challenges – Islamophobia; meeting a marriage partner

Chapter 2..43
Building Connections for Our Children

- Connection – parenting styles
- Connection to Allah
- Connection with the Self – building your child's self-esteem
- Connection with Family – communication; family traditions

Chapter 3..71
How and When to Talk About Sex

- Principles
- Sexual Development Needs of Children (how to support your child; tips for strengthening the parent-child bond)
- Puberty
- Menstruation
- Erections
- Nocturnal Emission (wet dream)
- Conception and Fertilization
- Contraception
- STIs – Sexually Transmitted Infections
- Masturbation
- Oral/Anal Sex
- Pornography
- Islamic view on Sexuality
- Pre-marital Sex in the Qur'an and Hadith
- Petting
- Halal Dating
- Love versus Infatuation
- Healthy Relationships

Conclusion..130
References..132

INTRODUCTION

Dreading it! I think that's what first comes to mind when we consider talking to our children about sex. It is hard for parents and children to think of one another as sexual beings, so the conversation is always a little awkward.

I remember starting junior high, aged 12-years-old, saddened by the fact that nobody was playing games in the playground. The fact that I was still interested in skipping and hopscotch seems a world away from 12-year-old Muslim youths asking me about oral sex and pornography. I've seen 12-year-olds in relationships, vaping, and some who've even faced school suspension for coming in under the influence of drugs. Times have changed.

I was teaching sex education in the UK, and one of the sessions included a condom demonstration. There were two hijabis in that session who participated minimally, probably due to shyness and modesty. However, at the end of the year, there were two students pregnant in that class, and they were the two Muslim girls. American Muslim organization, Heart Women & Girls state that sexual experimentation, sexual violence and marital challenges may result from the lack of open dialogue and education about sexual health in our Muslim communities.[1]

A friend's twin nephews in the UK were 11-years-old when someone from an outside agency came in and taught them some games to take out to the playground. They were meant to teach the games to their peers in order to combat the fact that this generation of children growing up with smartphones lacks in imaginative play. The internet is a fantastic tool, but it has come at a cost, especially for children and youth.

Parenting in the age of social media has presented parents with a whole new set of challenges, most notably the decline of moral values. We are living in the most sexualized time ever known and the generation gap experienced today is unlike any other time in history. It is even worse than when my children, now 22- and 24-years-old, were growing up. I remember trying very hard to preserve the childhood innocence of my sons against a tide pulling them in the opposite direction. I used to rent the series Little House on the Prairie and other similar shows and movies because they depicted decency and good morals. I also read books to them that did the same. However, I realized early on that you can't cocoon your children away from the worst parts of life.

Raising young children is physically demanding, and I remember thinking it would get easier as they got older. Yes, it's not as physically demanding, but it becomes more emotionally taxing. There are so many things tugging at us.

Questions like 'Am I doing okay with my parenting?' 'Why is my child becoming so rude?' 'How can I make sure they feel okay being Muslim?' 'How do I navigate the teen years when they want to do what others are doing?' 'Am I making life more difficult for them by saying no and opening them up to ridicule?' and 'How can I make them stop playing videogames all the time?' will dominate your thoughts.

Allah has blessed adolescents with curiosity. On a positive note, this is the age they become passionate about the environment or animal rights and become vegetarian or develop an interest in other important issues. On the negative side, this curiosity also makes them want to see naked bodies, know how it feels to 'get high' or 'drunk' or have a girlfriend/boyfriend.

There are so many things that cause inner conflict when raising children. We need to allow them to have a social life and also accept that the socializing cannot be controlled by a certain age. I did not allow any X-box/PlayStation games aside from sports or strategy games. However, when my sons were invited to birthday parties or to play at friends' homes, especially as they got older, I had less control over what they played or watched there. That feeling of helplessness was real. Once an image is seen, it can't be unseen. You may be taking care of what your children are watching, but it doesn't mean that other parents, including Muslims, are on the same page. I used to pay attention to ratings on videogames and movies but discovered that some parents did not.

When my sons were in elementary school, I always invited friends and parents over first to get to know them, and I did not hesitate to let the parents know my rules on TV and video games. Once my sons moved school, at 12 years of age, I no longer always knew the parents of their friends, and so found it more difficult to initiate these conversations. I feared my sons would be made fun of if I called the parents ahead of time to discuss my rules, and this resulted in them playing age-inappropriate games at friends' houses on occasion. I know this because they told me so. I would then remind them of the values portrayed in those games and how they aren't good for us. Unfortunately, I lacked the courage to call those parents and set boundaries for my children. As an antidote to this, I got my sons involved with sports and music lessons, which widened their social circles and kept them busy. When my sons were university bound, I asked them why they didn't have much interest in gaming and they responded that because they weren't allowed to play the games others were playing, they hadn't become addicted to gaming. Plus, they had developed other interests like playing sports and musical instruments.

When my son was at the end of Year 7 in the UK (equivalent to Grade 7 in Canada), the end of school movie was scheduled to be *John Tucker Must Die*. The name alone sounded suspect. John is a popular basketball player and serial cheater. Three girls he dated decide to teach him a lesson by having a new girl seduce and then dump him. Further antics are carried out to humiliate him. The theme of bullying is presented as entertainment.

In the movie, the high school girls wear skimpy clothing; one of them undresses in front of the camera for John; and boys wear thong underwear. There are some kissing and petting scenes, as well as references to STIs (sexually transmitted infections). Slang includes the word 'slut,' and 'uncork and pork,' referring to the boys' dating strategy. The most disturbing part is that the movie suggestion came from teachers at the school.

When I found out this was the movie of choice, I watched it and found it inappropriate. Boys are studs, girls are mean bullies, and the whole movie was sexually inappropriate. I phoned the school, and an administrator told me that I was the only parent that complained. I responded that other parents would assume that the school would show something age-appropriate, but I wouldn't take that for granted. Well, the principal took the movie home, watched it, and agreed with me. The movie was switched to *High School Musical*. This incident is an example of the fact that the wider society is not looking after the best interests of our children. You, parents, need to make yourselves aware and be your child's advocates.

I wish I had known more about how to parent in this era when I had my children. I began conversations too late. My sons should have grown up with the correct sexual language and a more open dialogue. It was only when my elder son went to Year 7 and asked me what masturbation and a 69 was that I realized they shouldn't be finding out about these topics outside our home. I assumed their dad was taking care of these difficult conversations, including pornography, but I should have checked in with them more often.

One year, my older son had to use the school bus. Secondary school in the UK begins at Year 7 and continues through to Year 12. That is a significant age spread between grades, and the conversations of those age groups are very different. I remember a work colleague in the UK telling me about the older kids showing the younger kids' porn on her son's school bus. I think back to that time and regret that, despite being forewarned, I didn't have a conversation with my son about porn. I passed it on to his father to have that conversation and assumed he had. I found out years later that he hadn't talked about it because he didn't feel comfortable or confident to do so. My younger son was 12-years-of-age when he was shown porn at school. He told me kids were using their phones to watch it and share sites and it was 'everyday teenage boy behaviour.' His older brother was also exposed to porn at school. Since neither their father nor I had spoken to them about porn, they had no way to process what they had seen and did not come and tell us about it. I only found out about their first initiation many years later by asking them.

I currently work in a junior high school with Grades 7-9 students, aged 12- to 14-years-old. Whenever sexual health lessons are to take place, the list of students to be excused from the sessions are mostly Muslim names, which doesn't surprise me. The same thing happened when we brought in an outside agency to do a presentation on cyberbullying, flirting, and sexual harassment. In my previous role, I conducted Healthy Relationships lessons in an Islamic school, and some children were entirely unaware of age-appropriate content and couldn't handle it. This response spoke to me of stigma and shame around this topic.

I listened to an interview recently with Farrah Marfatia, the principal of Maingate Islamic Academy in Toronto, where she spoke about sex education in schools. She mentioned that in 2013, 100% of the calls from Muslim boys aged 11- to 14-years-old to the Islamic helpline, Naseeha, were related to masturbation and pornography[2]. Just let that sink in for a moment: 100% of the calls.

Research by the UK based child protection charity NSPCC (National Society for the Prevention of Cruelty to Children) found that 53% of 11- to 16-year-olds have seen explicit material online. By age 14-years, 94%

of them had seen it[3]. We should assume our children are in that statistic because they likely are. Pornography is no longer the 'dirty magazine' hidden under a mattress. It is violent, deviant, graphic, anonymous and accessible at the click of a button.

Conversations around sex and relationships are absent in too many Muslim homes. There are many reasons Muslim parents are reluctant to discuss sex and sexuality with their children.

1. There is this perception in the Muslim community that if children learn about sex and sexuality, their awakening curiosity is going to lead to sexual activity.

2. Some Muslim parents fear that the values of the dominant culture will be adopted, which will be at odds with the family's cultural and religious values.

3. Some parents don't know what to say, how to say it, or when to say it. These parents may have been raised in homes that, for example, cloaked the concept of menstruation in secrecy, making this healthy bodily function seem shameful.

4. Some parents carry the misconception that their kids are too young to be given information about sex.

5. Muslim parents often believe that our children won't be at risk because they know that dating and pre-marital sex is haram.

The above-listed reasons for Muslim parents not discussing sex with their children are based on unfounded assumptions.

1. Comprehensive sex education programs do not increase sexual activity rates but are instead 'empowering young people with the tools to delay sex and make more responsible decisions.' [4]

2. Talking about sex to your kids is protective. Studies have shown that parents influence their teens' sexual behaviors in a positive way when they talk to them about sex.[5]

3. Our traditions of modesty make talking about sexual desires or menstruation seem unnatural, and so we have to remind ourselves that sex is a gift from our Creator, which means it is a good thing. We have to challenge ourselves to step outside our comfort zones. Over time, the discomfort is reduced, and it becomes much easier to have these conversations.

4. Children and youths are being brought into the adult world at younger ages than before and need guidance to navigate these turbulent years.

   By ensuring your kids understand boundaries, they will be better equipped to recognize situations that may be unsafe or make them feel uncomfortable. They will be able to talk to an adult about inappropriate touch without feeling shame.

5. The 'not my child' argument is naïve on the part of parents today. Sadly, the reality is that '... studies show that 2/3 of Muslims in Canada and the US admit to having sex before marriage, and at least 50% of those who hadn't, considered it.' [6] Knowing what's right doesn't stop someone from doing the wrong thing.

The good news is that teens want to talk to their parents about it. A teen survey found that almost 90% of teens '...said that it would be much easier to postpone sexual activity and avoid pregnancy if they were able to have more open, honest conversations about these topics with their parents.' [7]

Unfortunately, the majority of young Muslims reported most often receiving sexual health information from the media, and least often receiving it at home.[8]

There it is. Young Muslims want to have these conversations with parents at home, but that is where it is least likely to happen. Your children are taking in sexual language and imagery every day. It is in music and music videos, TV shows, billboards, magazines, commercials, and movies.

Even the word 'sexy' is overused and often used inappropriately. I recall a car advertisement that described a car as 'sexy.' When my son went away to university, I bought him a cookbook written by a teenager and marketed towards students. One of the recipes is 'sexy salmon,' a testament to sexual innuendo everywhere.

You probably give your children an allowance to teach them valuable lessons such as the value of money and patience so that they can learn how to save up for things, how to budget and delay gratification. Somehow with a crucial topic like sex, we don't guide them through the years like we guide them in how to use money. Sex is powerful. It can create a new life and completely change your life. Yes, we hope for the best and make du'a for our children. Continue to make du'a but also do for your children. Your children are getting exposure to sexually related and even explicit imagery at ever younger ages. If they aren't getting the information from you, they will get it from peers and from the internet where it is easy to stumble onto pornography.

It is completely understandable that parents want to protect their children, but they are doing their children a great disservice by not preparing them for the harsher parts of the world.

Talking to your children empowers and protects them! Many students attended the sessions I did with high schoolers on dating and relationships. Muslim teens are desperate for accurate information which is sensitive to their cultural and religious views. Simply telling them sex before marriage is haram is not keeping them abstinent. They need strong arguments against immorality. We should be teaching them that sex in Islam is something good that we have been given as a gift within a marriage. They need communication at home because their hormones are raging in a world filled with sexual imagery, leaving them at the mercy of society's different set of values.

They are subject to contradictory, confusing messages. On the one hand, sex is everywhere: magazine covers down the aisle at the grocery shop; at the mall; on billboards and TV; and in music. So, it must be important, because everybody wants to have sex. On the other hand, it's no big deal because you don't have to be committed to anyone to have sex. People on TV shows and movies hop into bed at the end of a first date, sometimes not even remembering their date's name in the morning!

Islam is not a religion of defeat. The decadence that surrounds us will have an impact on the spiritual health of our children, so we must step up to face it. In this book, I will show you how to provide that guidance that is so sorely needed. This information will help you stay one step ahead of your children so you can keep them on the right path, in shaa Allah.

The American Muslim organization, Heart Women & Girls, very effectively summarizes what will happen if the Muslim youth are not given good sex education. They state that the Muslim youth will be left unprepared and unequipped when it comes to reproductive and sexual health, and warn that the consequences of this abandonment are severe. These kids are left confused and curious, relying on outdated cultural traditions, or searching for answers from pornography or their peers, resulting in misinformation and unhealthy attitudes. The long-term effects of no sex education include poor decision making, such as succumbing to the pressure to engage in sexual activity because of a lack of understanding around the consequences of sex. A lack of sex education also puts kids at risk of failing to recognize what makes a healthy relationship and can result in not being able to recognize abuse and failing to seek help. They're also at an increased risk of an unhealthy marital sex life. [9]

In Islam, there are many instances recorded of the Prophet Muhammad (PBUH) treating children with gentleness and affection. There is a hadith related where a man told the Prophet that he had never kissed any of his ten children, to which the Messenger of Allah (PBUH) responded 'Whoever does not show mercy will not be shown mercy' (Sahih Muslim, Book 30, Hadith 5736).

Giving your children knowledge, I believe, is a form of mercy. Mercy is showing compassion to someone. If we can understand the immorality our children are exposed to, providing them with an Islamically based comprehensive sex education is an act of mercy, which is a tradition of our faith.

I want to include some sections from a shareable Facebook post from the UK based Shaykh Abu Eesa Niamatullah of Al-Maghrib Institute. This scholar also recognizes the seriousness of this issue, stating:

Our refusal to be mature about sexual taboos is going to cause a catastrophe amongst our youth, and bigger than the one it is in currently. You cannot avoid this. Your children *will* get to see and experience these matters WHATEVER you try and do.

I have made this my own personal crusade for many years now and as #ProtectThisHouse students will know, I don't aim to stop any time soon despite many parents not happy with my approach. See, Muslims believe that being super religious at home, or making their kids memorise all and sundry at madrasah, or sending them to Islamic schools, will somehow protect them against the prevailing sexual culture that dominates every aspect of life today. You should be shaking your head right now.

I can 100% guarantee to you that if you don't get into your children's minds before our modern-day culture does, you will lose them to that culture. We cannot blame the kids. We decided to bring them up here, we have to take responsibility.

And that means being close enough to them and personal enough with them so that they see you as their best friend, the one they intimately trust with *everything*, the one that they will turn to the second they feel strange about that boy or girl in school, the one they will turn to when they come across that porno clip on their friend's iPhone, the one they will come to explain what they saw happening behind the proverbial bike shed.

That's only going to happen if you are completely open with your children, if they feel you're not hiding anything from them, if they feel super comfortable with you and completely TRUST you. You must be their best friend. Because if you don't, there are hundreds of other children/adults/marketing executives willing to step in at the drop of a hat.[10]

Ultimately, we want to raise our children to be adults who can enjoy and sustain a mutually satisfying, healthy relationship in marriage. If we want to achieve this goal, then we must build those relationship skills from birth and guide our children to handle their sexuality Islamically.

Having spent 20 years teaching and working with pre-teens, teens and young adults, I want to equip you with tools that will help you gain the confidence to have these conversations by

- opening a general channel of communication with your child/children; and

- helping you to understand what age-appropriate information they need.

This book will include:

Chapter 1 -
The Challenge of Raising Children in a Digital World

Chapter 2 -
Building Connections for Our Children

Chapter 3 -
How and When to Talk About Sex

Islam has a history of openness about sexuality and the education around it. The Qur'an mentions menstruation, conception, ejaculation, and the sexual rights of both men and women. Prophet Muhammad (PBUH) spoke to the ummah about these matters. He did not shy away from them. We are born sexual beings. A healthy sexual education is necessary, and it is Islamically appropriate to provide that information. Islam doesn't have hang-ups, parents do.

Your children need you to step out of your comfort zone. I will remove your stress and reduce your discomfort about dealing with these sensitive topics by outlining what you need to teach and how you need to guide your children concerning sex and sexuality.

THE CHALLENGE OF RAISING CHILDREN IN A DIGITAL WORLD

You are the most critical influence in your child's life. You are going to shape your child's values, beliefs, and character through a healthy and connected parent-child relationship. Never underestimate this.

It's essential to start with the challenges of raising a child in the West and in a digitalized world. Parents need to be aware of the environment our children are being exposed to from the media and peers so we can anticipate the guidance that they'll need. This awareness allows you to be proactively supportive of their needs. I will be frank in this section because I don't think many parents are aware of just how low the bar has dropped. We cannot remain in the dark or in denial.

Knowledge is power, and in Islam, we are expected to seek knowledge from the cradle to the grave. The more you know and understand of your child's world and of youth culture, the easier it will be for you to correctly influence and guide them. My 20-years-worth of workdays in the company of youths and teens have given me invaluable insight into their world that you need to cultivate. This insight should also increase your empathy for how difficult it must be for your children to be surrounded by immorality.

Even our Islamic scholars are recognizing the reality of raising children today and the unique challenges that come with it. I listened to Shaykh Yasir Qadhi's YouTube lecture on 'Raising Teenagers in a World of Pornography, Drugs, and Pre-marital Sex.' He raised some important points for us parents to consider. If we keep our kids in an ultra-conservative bubble with too much protection, when they go off to college and the bubble bursts, they're thrown in the deep end because they haven't been prepared for real life.

There is no easy answer. You cannot keep your child innocent and naïve until 17. We must find the middle ground. The threat of punishment is not enough. Young people are leaving Islam and have no fear of Allah. Shaykh Yasir shared two different incidents of antisocial behaviour. In the first instance, groups of Muslim teens (boys and girls) were in the masjid parking lot smoking weed, while their parents were praying Tarawih. A teen told him it was happening, so he went outside and saw them. One of them even complimented him on his lecture. The second occurred at one of his talks where a teenage Muslim drug dealer used it as an opportunity to sell drugs to youths in the masjid parking lot.

He mentioned some parents had removed their television to control media exposure, but that removing a TV doesn't stop children from going to friends and neighbors and watching TV where you have no control over it and can't monitor them. Shaykh Yasir's family opted not to have broadcast TV and to use subscription services instead.

Our job as parents is to minimize the threats our children are surrounded by because we cannot isolate them from it. Parents can't be naïve and think 'not my son,' or 'not my daughter.' Your sons and daughters are just as exposed as anyone else's son or daughter. Children know much more than you think. They have countless opportunities to access all kinds of inappropriate content. It is, therefore, essential to be available to our children to answer questions. You have created a problem if they are too scared to come to you because they have been shut down by your reactions or been made to feel shame about such information.

Shaykh Yasir further stated that it is not Islamic to spy on your kids, so let them know that the computer is monitoring their activities and use software to block pornography. With Facebook, he suggested you have access to the password until they are older, at which point you become their Facebook friend. Check in with your kids about whether or not they are okay with you commenting on their posts. My sons did not have internet access on their phones till their late teens, and parental controls were enabled on the home computer and their devices.

As children approach the teenage years, they will want more privacy, as my sons did. They may start keeping their bedroom doors closed and giving you less information about what's going on in their lives. This desire for privacy is a natural part of growing up and should be respected within reasonable limits. It would be unreasonable for your child to put a lock on the door preventing you access, for example.

He reminds us to educate, reinforce and make children aware that Allah is watching, so they're motivated to not cross the red line. Negotiate instead of using the stick. Do not be tyrannical, which breeds resentment. Also, cut them some slack; they will make mistakes here and there. Allow their minor errors so you can guide them to avoid making the big mistakes.

During Shaykh Yasir Qadhi's lecture on 'Raising Teenagers in a World of Pornography, Drugs, and Pre-marital Sex,' he concluded with the following:

- Never underestimate the power of Du'a. Religious values, morals, and ethics must come from you. You set the bar. Live the life that you want your child to live because 'He who does not live in the way of his beliefs starts to believe in the way he lives' (Umar ibn Al-Khattab).

- Don't think that a once-a-month Islamic lecture or visit to the masjid is doing enough. Model a healthy relationship between spouses. Even if your children go astray, as long as they are raised in a healthy Islamic home, they will come back to those values in their adult life. This return may even be after marrying and wanting to start a family because they've seen that it works.

Lastly, he implored parents to have conversations about drugs, pornography, and sex by junior high (12- to 14-years) because you don't want the media and peers giving your children information before you can.[11]

PICK YOUR BATTLES

You must pick your battles carefully. Brain development is not complete until the early to mid-20s, so our teens are sometimes going to be impulsive and will not always make the right decisions. During adolescence, the brain gets rewired, and you can expect them to be hypersensitive, emotional, and irrational during arguments. What is important to you may not be relevant to them.

Richard Carlson wrote a book titled *Don't Sweat the Small Stuff...and it's all Small Stuff*, the chief philosophy of which can be simplified as let go of the smaller battles. Many teens want to keep up with the latest fashion trends which is an unfortunate emulation of pop culture. When my son was between 12 and 14 years, he wanted the newest hairstyle and to add vibrant color to his hair. He also expressed an interest in getting his ears pierced and having a tattoo. He wore a chunky chain for a brief spell, as well.

I wasn't happy with any of these choices, but I didn't overreact. I let him talk about what he found desirable about these choices. I then spoke about the Islamic perspective on ear piercing, tattoos, and jewelry without turning it into a lecture. I was clear that as Muslims, we don't imitate the opposite gender in our appearance. My son was trying to express himself as well as assert some independence and control in his life. In the end, he only ended up changing his hairstyle. He never added color, pierced his ears, or got a tattoo, and eventually he stopped wearing his chunky chain. We wouldn't have allowed tattoos or ear piercings, but we didn't even have to tell him that because feeling heard was enough to satisfy him, which opened his mind and made him receptive to hearing my message and then make the right choice. Let your teens feel they have some control over the smaller battles, so they don't rebel when it comes to the more significant matters.

It can be difficult when parents favour different parenting styles. Before my sons were born, I told my husband at the time that I did not want spanking to be used to discipline our children, and he agreed. I was fortunate that he let me take the lead in terms of parenting style. He knew I had read many books on parenting, attended courses and workshops, and had completed several university courses on child psychology and development. The best way to deal with a spouse who is on a different page to you with regards to parenting is to seek knowledge. Read books or articles on parenting to make a case for your viewpoint. It will be difficult for your spouse to argue against the advice of an expert in child development and effective parenting.

CULTURAL NORMS

My sister, a mother of three adult children, was, like many parents, not aware of how vulgar the media has become. When I showed her some current music videos and song lyrics, she was shocked. The shift in cultural mores is real. Getting drunk and trying drugs is normal; premarital sex is a given; cohabitation before marriage is sensible, and violent video games are entertainment.

Let's start by accepting the fact that our children are North American or European or whatever nationality, who happen to be Muslim. I am not discounting their Muslim identity, but the overarching environment they grow up in will have an impact on them culturally and socially. They want to fit in. They want to belong, which is a need all human beings possess. It is much harder to resist this urge as a child or youth.

American Muslim youths do not feel that their parents understand youth culture. There is a hadith that tells parents, 'Do not force your own customs upon your children for they are in other times than yours' (Ali RA). This does not mean parents have to give up their culture, but they must understand that their children may not share their cultural needs and interests. Parents can become unduly strict because of their concerns around their child's reputation and assimilation in the dominant culture.

The problem with being too strict is that you could be setting the stage for rebellion, which will be done without your knowledge. I've spoken to Muslim girls who felt so stifled because they were not allowed to do normal teenage things, like go to the mall or a movie with friends, that they chose to attend university as far away from their parents as possible. Sometimes children also lead double lives, having a dutiful home persona and a very different outside-the-house one. I've met both personas many a time. I taught a Muslim girl who would come to college with her hijab, then take it off in the bathroom and make herself look 'sexy' to send photos to boys. I didn't recognize her the first time I saw the images. Our children are not going to disclose everything about their lives to us, but we don't want them having two very different personalities either.

The experiences of Muslim children and youths growing up today is going to be very different to those of their parents.

They will have classmates who identify as gay or transgender at younger ages than their parents ever had. In my son's first year at university, he lived in a student hall with someone who was transitioning from male to female. In my schooling years, I never knew anyone who was homosexual, bisexual, trans or any of the other labels on the spectrum of sexuality that now exist.

Your children will be growing up with very different experiences that will shape their worldview. They will not respond well to your accounts of 'well when I was your age ...' because their different context won't allow them to appreciate the point you are making. Sometimes these differences are even beneficial. Youths nowadays are less racist than their parents' generation. Sometimes too much 'cultural' baggage can get in the way of Islam, which our youth don't carry. I was mentoring a Pakistani Muslim student teacher who met a fellow Pakistani Muslim at university. They were desperate to get married, but it took them two years to convince their parents to give them their blessing because they came from different tribes. This young couple did not relate to their parents' generation's tribal mentality.

PEER ORIENTATION

There is a growing phenomenon called peer attachment. This is where children become more attached to their peers than to the adults in their lives. This can start in young children since we see greater and longer periods of separation from parents due to issues such as divorce, economic needs and no extended family. When the need for contact and closeness is being met by peers, parents lose their influence and the child is more likely to be led astray into drugs, alcohol and sexual activity. Peer oriented children move away from parental values and become defiant and difficult. Our children at school may be mean, bully others, make poor choices, crack dirty jokes, swear and act quite differently with their friends than when they are with us. They are taking their cues from their peers and seeking out to meet their attachment needs from them as well. Peer oriented kids are those who want to fit in, those who copy and are always trying to please their friends, those same friends who may be fickle and veer from niceness to nastiness at any time. It is through adult attachments, however—not peers—that they will learn to grow up to be socially competent respectful adults.[12]

SEX-OBSESSED CULTURE

We live in a sex-obsessed culture that is removing the innocence of children at an alarming rate. Western culture mentality is all about 'if it feels good do it' because you only live once (YOLO) and attaches to everything the fear of missing out (FOMO).

Sex is everywhere and has no morality attached to it. This sacred gift from Allah is dishonored. The book *Fifty Shades of Grey* was called 'mummy porn' because it appealed to a broad spectrum of women, including mothers. Its soft-porn movie version, which explored BDSM (Bondage & Discipline or Dominance & Submission or Sadism & Masochism), was mainstream. It received an R rating, but when I was growing up, this would have been X-rated. Even Muslim high schoolers have read the books and romanticized the relationship between the main characters. When the movie came out, I opened a class discussion to talk about it (despite having not read the book nor seen the movie) to point out the terrible message given by the film. I read a few articles written by psychologists about this movie and discussed it with colleagues who had seen the movie, so I felt confident in my ability to address this.

It was alarming that these impressionable high schoolers couldn't see the fact that there was nothing healthy in the relationship between the two main characters. A billionaire begins a relationship with a virgin and introduces her to his world of BDSM. She is controlled, degraded, and abused but is portrayed to enjoy a great lifestyle.

Even if your child has never read the books or watched the movies, your child may not be able to avoid conversations about popular culture phenomenon's like these with other youngsters.

Sexualization of Children

The sexualization of children, particularly girls, is getting worse. There are beauty pageants for little girls where they wear heavy make-up, heels, and bathing suits. Dolls for young girls are wearing inappropriate clothing like fishnet stockings.

Young girls have to wear heavy make-up to their ballet recitals. They wear midriff-baring tops or bralettes in dancing competitions while dancing suggestively. Six-year-olds compete in salsa dancing championships. Children are in the adult world where they don't belong.

Young children are listening to age-inappropriate music. On the Ellen show, a 6-year-old girl and her younger friend performed a Nicki Minaj song and then met the hip-hop artist. Minaj's song lyrics are profane and sexually explicit, which raises two questions: 1) Why was this behavior celebrated and applauded on a TV show as cute and appropriate? 2) Why have her parent(s) allowed her to listen to Nicki Minaj and imitate her? Society at large is not looking after children.

In schools, I've seen Grade 7 (equivalent to Year 7 in the UK) girls wearing make-up and sporting manicured false nails while some of the Grade 9s have exposed midriffs, worn low-cut tops, and short shorts. At the year-end dance, there were 12- to 14-year-old girls wearing stilettos with a range of transparent, strapless, and backless dresses. These are the peers of our children. I remember my nephew talking about how embarrassed he felt sometimes because of how the girls came dressed to school. He didn't know where to look! As Canadian schools move to a more 'student-centered' dress code, this will be the new norm. In Islam, modesty is for men and women, so we also need to talk to our sons about their modesty as well.

A study found that when presented with a 'sexy doll' and a covered up stylish doll, 6- to 9-year-old girls most often chose the sexy doll. There was an association with sexiness and popularity.[13] I have seen girls in this age group posing for photos with their hands on their hips or wearing make-up and trying to look coquettish. Girls' clothing is sexualized through skimpiness or slogans such as 'hot stuff', 'foxy' and so on, and thong underwear is even available for pre-teens. The impact of this early sexualization, as reported by the American Psychological Association, is that young girls will be more likely to experience low self-esteem, depression, and eating disorders.[14]

Teen Vogue, which has a readership of mainly 13- to 17-year-olds, published a list of 'best' back to school items. The 2017 list included: items for self-pleasure and a sex-ed book that 'challenges heteronormative standards about getting down.' Their November 2019 issue had a guide to anal sex to ensure you know how to do it the right way! This is the content in a 'teen' magazine![15]

Sexualization through Music and Music Videos

This sexualization has spilled over into music too. Even if you believe music is haram, that doesn't mean your children aren't listening to it. Music plays in the classroom, at assemblies and school events, and students can sometimes listen to their music while doing computer work. I've seen it. I work with a Grade 8 student who is not allowed to listen to music at home but loves listening to music at school while practicing her dance moves. Sometimes music is played loudly during the school lunch hour, including songs with bleeped-out profanity or inappropriate sexual content. The song 'Rude Boy' by Rihanna was being played during the track and field day at a junior high/middle school while the students were lining up for lunch. The entire song is about a sexual experience, and it was hard to avoid hearing it. Rihanna's song 'S&M,' which mentions sex in the air and chains and whips, was also freely allowed on mainstream radio.

When I was growing up in the 70s and 80s, you never had to worry about the lyrics of songs on the radio. Nowadays, swearing and explicit language is normalized in music, even by mainstream artists.

Pop stars like Disney-kid-show alumni Miley Cyrus, Ariana Grande and Demi Lovato—who all have a young fan base—all use F-bombs in their songs. Their dance routines are highly sexualized and their outfits, skimpy. They wear underwear as outerwear. Their Instagram pages are full of provocative selfies. Many young girls, including young Muslims, look up to these poor role models. The boys I've worked with are more into hip-hop songs, which have profanity, highly sexualized content, and videos that objectify women.

Ariana Grande's 'Side to Side,' a pop song where she is 'making deals with the devil,' is about having so much sex you can't walk straight. Girls as young as eight-years-old, some of them Muslim, attended her UK concerts.

Kids are being influenced by what they hear. Katy Perry sings about kissing a girl and liking it. Demi Lovato sings about a same-sex summer fling. After breaking up with her boyfriend, a secondary school student in the UK came to me and said, 'I think I will give girls a try,' because the message is that sexual orientation is fluid and can be confirmed only through experimentation. I've noticed that more students over the years have disclosed to me that they are bisexual or confused about their sexual orientation.

Recently, I asked a Grade 7 girl what her favorite song was because they had to do a dramatic reading of a song. She said, 'I can't tell you because it's inappropriate; it's a rap song with bad words.' Kids are not downloading the clean versions of songs either. Some Muslim teens told me that they want to hear songs in their original form, meaning explicit, unedited versions.

Music videos have added another layer of vulgarity to music. When kids like a song, they like to see the accompanying music video which can now feature nudity, profanity and violence, and still land at the top of the charts.

Clean versions of songs sit alongside the explicit versions on YouTube. I looked at a couple of songs and compared their clean vs. explicit versions for the number of views. The graphic versions were more popular by the millions! These are just a click away for our children. Sadly, this is the culture of popular music nowadays.

I used to check my sons' playlists and continued to remind them that their ears will give testimony against them on the Day of Judgement, so they should make good choices. The Qur'an tells us in surah 24, verse 24 that 'On the Day when their tongues, their hands, and their feet will bear witness against them as to their actions.' I also used to get my sons to think about how they spent their time by asking 'are you binge watching TV series after TV series? Think about what you are filling your mind with. What are your ears hearing? What are your eyes watching? These are the windows to our soul. Is there anything good in it or is it bad? This ultimately affects your spiritual heart and can bring you closer to Allah or move you further away.'

Sexualization in TV and Movies

A 2018 Canadian study found on average that 8- to 11-year-old children spent 3.6 hours per day on a TV, mobile phone, tablet, or computer screen, nearly double the two-hour suggested limit.[16] TV has changed a lot over the years. I grew up with clean family shows that the whole family could watch. It is much harder to find family shows nowadays because two out of every three TV shows include sexual content.[17] Netflix has brought swearing, sex, and nudity into primetime and into our living rooms. The culture of disrespect is huge. The way youths speak to parents is an example of this. I watched something recently where a 17-year-old kid said to his parents, 'I need a f***ing car,' and then he was given a car. Parents are portrayed as out of touch buffoons who deserve little respect. A former work colleague used to accept her children calling her by her first name and swearing in front of her. My sons used to tell me that it was quite normal for their friends to speak to their parents rudely. Do not accept disrespect. Remind them that the Qur'an surah 17 verse 23, states 'Your Lord has decreed that ye worship none but Him, and that ye be kind to parents.'

When I was growing up, an F-bomb in a movie garnered an R-rating, which is no longer the case. When the movie Terminator first came out, its rating suggested viewers should be at least 18-years-old. Now, that age has dropped to 12. More violence, sexual content, and profanity are now allowed in movies that children are watching than in the past.

Limits and regular conversations about what your children are watching are needed. I always talked with my boys about our accountability to Allah and how we spend our time. At some point, it was no longer within my control, but I continued to provide reminders so that the message still got heard.

Netflix is not restricted by the Federal Communications Commission's (FCC) guidelines on indecent or profane material because it is a subscription service. The problem with this is that teens watch Netflix twice as much as they do cable. [18]

Popular TV shows that pre-teens and teens enjoy include *Friends* and *Glee*. Although both of these shows have now ended, they do appeal to youths. In *Friends*, the character Joey is constantly looking to have sex—with anyone. Although *Glee* is set in a high school, it does not promote family values. Over time the storylines became more sexually inappropriate, dance routines became more seductive, and same-sex characters were seen making out.

When my sons were in secondary school in the UK, their peers used to watch *Skins* and *The Inbetweeners*, both containing profane and sexually explicit content.

I recently had a class discussion with Grade 7s on their favorite TV shows, and the names that came up were *Stranger Things*, *Family Guy*, and *On My Block*.

Stranger Things is a show where they 'swear a lot,' according to a Muslim boy who watches it. *Family Guy* is meant for an adult audience, and *On My Block*, although geared towards a middle school audience, contains questionable content. There is a masturbation scene, a close-up of a teen's bouncing breasts, drug use, drinking, references to oral sex, and some swear words. Muslim kids are also watching this show. It's essential to sit down and watch whatever your children are viewing so you can talk about the content. I've spelled this out, in order to make it clear that parents shouldn't think viewing is safe simply because the characters are similar ages to your children.

A recent Vanity Fair article described some explicit Netflix comedies about the struggles of puberty as ground-breaking.[19] The latest offerings include:

Big Mouth, an animated show set in a middle school, making it seem innocent, while it is actually profane and sexually explicit.

Sex Education, set in a UK Sixth Form (16- to 17-year-olds), revolves around a shy 16-year-old who lives with his sex therapist mother. He sets up an underground business at school as a sex therapist. This sexually explicit show is full of f-words and vulgar slang. There is nudity and simulations of sexual acts. The sex therapist mother engages in casual sex with different partners, as do the students. Sadly, this show has been praised for being sex-positive.

Why am I telling you about these vulgar shows? I want to remind you that we lose control over our children's viewing choices by a certain age, and they are still affected by what they watch. A 2014 American study looked at media consumption for 14- to 21-year-olds. Only 2% of youths whose media consumption had minimal to no sexual content engaged in sexual activity. Meanwhile, 60% of youth whose media consumption mostly or always contained sexual content engaged in sexual activity.[20] There is a relationship between exposure to sexual content in the media and sexual activity, so it would be prudent to have plenty of conversations with your children about healthy relationships and healthy sexuality.

Where has Pop Culture Landed?

Changing social norms have allowed teen content to become more explicit. Whereas the movies of the 80s and 90s were all about losing your virginity, these new shows are so graphic, they are described in the above-mentioned Vanity Fair article as 'unlike anything we've seen before'.

A 2016 Facebook post by Shaykh Omar Suleiman reminds us that though nudity and sexual activity are becoming more mainstream on cable and satellite networks, this doesn't mean it isn't pornography just because it isn't called that.

Another hit with teens was the Netflix original series *13 Reasons Why*, which explained a high-school girl's suicide. The series managed to start conversations around bullying, loneliness, and mental health, but the glimpse into teenage high-school life was one of casual sex, drinking, and drugs. The series had strong language throughout and a lot of sexual content.

We can't think that our children are not influenced or affected by what they watch. In April 2017, a month after this show premiered, teen suicides increased by nearly 30%, and March also had higher than expected rates, according to a study.[21] It doesn't prove causation, but there is a correlation. In light of this, the suicide scene is no longer in the series.

The titles of 'teen' movies such as *The Kissing Booth*, *Mean Girls*, and *Friends with Benefits* speak to the values of our society, and they are not favorable.

Most TV shows and movies are now at the complete opposite end of Islamic values and gaining mainstream acceptance. You may not be letting your children watch these shows, but many children are getting a steady diet of vulgarity, profanity, and sexual promiscuity despite that. You may think your child is safe from this because they are at an Islamic school. They are not. They may have friends, cousins or neighbors who go to regular schools, and they talk. Swearing and dating are also happening in Islamic schools. Our children do not live in bubbles, especially since they have smartphones. They are more aware than you think. Even if your children are not watching these TV shows, they may be influenced by other children who are watching them. If your children have laptops or TVs in their bedrooms, do you always know what they are watching or doing? Here is what they are doing: 57% of teens are searching for porn at least monthly, and 71% of them hide their online behavior from their parents.[22] Teens are deleting their browser histories, minimizing their screens when their parents walk in, blocking their parents using social media privacy settings, setting up new email or social media accounts unknown to parents, and using their phones instead of a computer. According to Google Analytics, porn searching increases 4700% when kids are out of school.[23]

TV shows are not going to align with our religious and moral values, so use them as teachable moments to express your values. Make yourself aware of what they are watching. There are websites such as https://www.commonsensemedia.org/ and https://kids-in-mind.com/ that will rate the content of TV shows and movies for parents. Sit down and watch a TV show with your pre-teens and teens, then discuss the content with them. Ask them to describe what is portrayed and explain why we might have an issue with this.

Profanity

It is not surprising that some Muslim kids are also swearing because they, too, have become desensitized by how common it is. I have even heard profanity in Islamic schools. By Grade 7, swearing is common. A Grade 8 Muslim boy I work with is profane and often indulges in sexually inappropriate conversations. According to him, 'swearing is the best way to fit in.' I was helping a new Grade 8 Muslim boy, who came from an Islamic school, with Math. The other two Grade 8 non-Muslim boys were trying to engage him in a very inappropriate conversation, and I could see his discomfort. I addressed the conversation, but since he has become friends with these two boys, his behavior has changed. He is trying to fit in and is also engaging in inappropriate conversations. Youths and teens are easily influenced. I recently spoke with a group of Grade 8 boys about swearing. One of them told me, 'we're in junior high now. I guarantee you that every single person in this school swears.' They further stated that you have to swear, especially when you play Fortnite. Parents need to be aware that players can talk and type whatever they want to each other, and apparently, swearing is rampant. I recently accompanied Grade 9s on a camping trip and swearing was common there too.

Profane and explicit lyrics are so normalized for young people that a hijabi DJ was playing songs containing both at a themed party I attended last year organized by Muslim university students. I've seen 'WTF' used on PowerPoint presentations while attending a Health Symposium. There was a recent radio ad by Volkswagen which contained two instances of profanity. The ad included 'what the' followed by a bleep as well as 'it's "bleeping" sweet' where it was evident what word they were omitting. What a shame that a company known for its family-style cars is stooping to this level of advertising.

I was quite clear with my sons as they were growing up that they were going to be surrounded by bad language, but they could make a choice. I always brought accountability to Allah into our conversations. 'I don't think the angels want to listen to swearing, do they?' 'Doesn't Prophet Muhammad say believers don't swear?' When my son let an F-bomb out in a moment of anger, I let him cool down completely and then said, 'If you think about what an F-bomb means, it is taking a blessing from

Allah and turning it into something vulgar, which Allah isn't going to be pleased with.' I also reminded them of the Sahih Hadith where Ibn Mas'ud reported: 'The Messenger of Allah, peace, and blessings be upon him said: "The believer does not insult others, does not curse others, is not vulgar, and is not shameless"' (Sunan al-Tirmidhī 1977). This encouraged a pause for reflection without shaming.

Despite this vulgarity, parents, 'Do not lose heart nor fall into despair! You shall triumph if you are believers' (Quran 3:139). Prophet Muhammad (PBUH) lived in a time surrounded by unbelievers, corruption, cruelty, idol worship, infanticide, drunkenness, gambling, and promiscuity.

It is possible to raise compassionate and God-conscious children through seeking Allah's help while you put the practical advice in this book to good use, in shaa Allah.

GENDER-SPECIFIC ISSUES

Some issues are specific to gender, and it is necessary to talk to both our sons and our daughters about the objectification of girls, and the 'boys will be boys' mentality which rationalizes toxic masculinity.

Girls

Throughout my career as an educator, the two most common struggles teen girls disclosed to me were disliking their appearance and struggling with low self-esteem. The constant comparisons to others have created unattainable standards of beauty. I had created a Facebook page for my Sixth Form (high school) students in the UK so that I could keep in touch with them as a class. The first time I went on there, I didn't recognize some of them because of the filters, pouts, and poses they displayed. Girls are creating their Facebook personas, which are not necessarily at all similar to them in real life. Society is telling these girls they are not good enough. We have to work on raising kids that reject that message. Raising their taqwa (God-consciousness) will help to remind them that we are here to please Allah, not other people.

Posts on Facebook or Instagram are all about getting likes and comments. Selfie after selfie is posted where friends try to outdo each other with the compliments. Girls are looking for constant reassurance, and the compliments they receive are defining their friendships and self-worth. They are uncomfortable with being themselves, resulting in body image issues. Body image issues also affect boys though not to the same extent as girls. Appearing masculine is important, and my sons, who were on the skinny side, worked out regularly to 'bulk up'. Cyberbullying and social media contribute to this insecurity and body image issues.

The pressure on girls to be sexy, send nudes, and perform oral sex, all while safeguarding their reputation, is real. Girls are called a tease if they aren't willing to have sex because boys are stereotyped to always want sex and thrills. The 'sexy selfie' culture for girls and the violent video-gaming for boys are the result.

The next chapter will discuss helping our children develop their self-esteem so they can reject these damaging standards and this behavior.

Boys

Toxic masculinity has put substantial pressure on boys to act cool and masculine and to be emotionally strong all the time. From a young age, boys get the message that 'big boys don't cry,' and they need to toughen up. There are still enduring cultural norms and clichés which stereotype boys and encourage them to 'sow their wild oats' and man up. Whether in TV, movies, video games, or music videos, it is always the females who are provocatively dressed, degraded, objectified, or there as eye candy for the males' benefit. This will not likely get better as the sexual content in video games has been steadily increasing.

What attitudes towards women and sexuality are boys learning? What message of respect towards women are young boys getting?

If my sons and I came across a sexually inappropriate image or ad while walking past a store or a billboard, it became a teachable moment. I would always have a conversation about it with my sons by stating something along the lines of: 'Do you think it's okay for a woman to show her body like that? This is done to get boys and men to stare at her. We should be asking ourselves, "Would Allah be pleased with this picture/image/ad/billboard?" Our bodies are not meant to be on display like that. We are meant to be modest and work on being beautiful on the inside. These pictures are all about making us believe that the most important thing about a woman is how she looks. That's why Allah tells us to lower our gaze and not stare at this. Lots of advertising uses sexual images, like flaunting someone's body, to sell things. Sex doesn't belong on a poster, billboard, bedroom wall, T-shirt, or calendar; it is a special gift from Allah for married people.' I added in a comment about the need to respect girls and not use language such as she's 'hot' or take part in conversations that refer to the anatomy of girls. Our body is something sacred and special from Allah so deserves to be honored.

It is helpful for boys to have good role models and mentors in their lives. My sons had no Muslim friends growing up until they were in their late teens. They do have three older male cousins who are great role models for them because they are practicing Muslims. I always encouraged my sons to have regular contact with these cousins by spending time with them during Ramadan and going on holidays with them. I believed it would influence my sons positively to see older boys holding on to their values, and it did.

Desensitization caused by gaming

Since boys play video games more often and for more extended periods of time than girls, this is a more pressing issue for parents of boys. The boys I work with mostly play their current favorite game, Fortnite.

There are many mothers of young boys in a Muslim Facebook group I'm in who are allowing their sons to play the game. The usual arguments were presented, such as 'I'm close by,' 'They have a time limit,' 'They know it's only a game,' and 'They know it's not real life.' There was also the odd comment that video games help math skills and response times. The New Zealand mosque shootings were live streamed by the shooter wearing a camera on top of his head and recording from the same perspective or role that your son would be playing, where he is going around shooting and killing people. How does that fit in with Islamic values?

I have seen the effect of these games on school performance. I've seen boys come to school exhausted because they have been gaming till late. They have difficulty maintaining focus.

Leonard Sax, the author of the excellent books *Boys Adrift, Girls on the Edge, Why Gender Matters* and *The Collapse of Parenting*, writes that there are 'studies showing that playing video games excessively undermines school performance, increases distractibility, and erodes the parent-child relationship. And, playing video games where the objective is to kill people - games such as Fortnite - over time, desensitizes gamers to violence. The American Academy of Pediatrics has concluded that games "in which killing others is the central theme"– a good summary of Fortnite – "are not appropriate for children." Incidentally, "children" here refers to "humans under 18 years of age." In their latest guidelines, the Academy advised that "Video games should not use human or other living targets or award points for killing" and that parents should not allow their kids to play games which violate this guideline. In case you haven't seen it, Fortnite is a game in which the object of the game is to kill other humans.'[24]

For a project at a junior high school, the kids had to watch the movie The Hunger Games and then complete a worksheet based on the film. I found this profoundly disturbing. The movie rating suggests it is age-appropriate for 14 years of age (younger viewers require an accompanying adult). It was played for 12-year-olds. The most worrisome part is the plot. One boy and one girl between the ages of 12 and 18 from each of 12 districts are selected to participate in the Hunger Games, a fight to the death which is televised for all to see. The entire movie is 24 participants trying to kill each other and be the last one standing. We have become so desensitized to violence that it is even seeping into our school curriculum.

While I was living in the UK, I remember watching a program about a study done with two groups of 12-year-old boys. One group played sports-related video games, and the second watched news footage of war.

A psychologist then interviewed these boys. The psychologist had a jar of pencils/pens on his desk, which he knocked over onto the floor, making it appear as if it were an accident. All the boys that had watched the sports video games stood up and picked up the pencils/pens. None of the boys who watched the war footage did. If empathy can be reduced in such a short amount of time, what is Fortnite doing to your son?

I want to ask parents to consider this: you are raising the next generation of men. Are you okay with your son playing games that do not help him in any way to become a more caring, empathic individual?

I kept technology away from my sons for as long as possible. It was easier to do so because they attended a Steiner/Waldorf school where there are no computers in primary school, and technology is discouraged until children are older. They didn't have TVs in their bedrooms. They didn't watch any TV before they were toddlers, and then once we introduced it, there were strict time limits. I read a lot of books about technology and its detrimental effects on a developing brain and the possibility that it can delay a child's expressive language. I remember my sister, a kindergarten teacher, telling me that she could always tell which kids watch television in the morning before they come to school because of the effect on their concentration and focus. I also kept to a 'TV only on weekends' rule until my sons were 8 and 10 respectively. One day my younger son went to put the TV on, and the older one said, 'Turn it off, it's not the weekend.' I was quite pleased with myself in that moment.

When my sons were young teens, they wanted to play Call of Duty because everyone at school was playing the 18+ game. I couldn't always control the fact that they might play it at someone else's house, but I could control what happened in my own home. It was simple. 'No, you cannot play that game in our home. It goes against my values as a human being and as a Muslim. I'm sorry you are sad about it, but I won't change my mind because I love you.' I honored my values while teaching my children essential lessons like delaying gratification, handling what they would deem unfair situations, and living with boundaries. Parents are struggling to say no. It takes courage. I just told my sons that this was not good. Yes, we had the odd moments of tears, and sometimes they felt left out, but they survived. I sat with them when the tears came and said 'I know you were hoping I would change my mind, but I simply cannot allow something which has nothing good in it. You will understand this when you are older. I'm sorry it may be hard for you at school, but you will be okay.' When they were older, they understood and told me I was a responsible parent.

Saying no to TV or video games should mean saying yes to board games, puzzles, bowling, or doing an activity together. If your child is addicted to gaming, you are going to have to work at setting limits then gently reconnecting and nurturing your relationship with them. The more time kids spend playing video games, the less positive attitudes they have toward their parents.[25]

A grade 9 boy told me he had clocked 1000 hours on Fortnite, like it was a badge of honor. But the truth is, the lack of outdoor time and free play is impacting the physical and mental health of our youth. Childhood obesity has become an issue because children and teens have become more sedentary. When you drive by parks, they are often empty or have just a few kids playing.

Children and young people are losing their conversational and face-to-face social skills. I taught teens for many years on an Early Childcare and Education course, and as part of the program, the students had to spend time in preschools, daycares, and schools where they would gain professional skills. I was astonished that 16-year-olds were unable to articulate on their own: 'Good morning. I'm so and so, and I am scheduled to come in and do a placement with you starting on this date. Can I book a visit to come in and introduce myself?' I had to write a script out for them to use when phoning their placement settings. They were getting tongue-tied without a reference to help them.

Dr. Sax recommends that parents set reasonable limits around video games and recommends these evidence-based guidelines for your son or daughter playing video games:

- 'No more than 40 minutes a night on school nights.

- No more than an hour a day on weekends.

- Your minutes do not roll over: if you go three weeks without playing, that does NOT mean that you can spend seven hours on a Saturday playing video games. That's binge gaming, and it is harmful.

- No games where the objective is to kill people. That means no Fortnite, no Call of Duty, no Grand Theft Auto. NBA Live is fine. Wii Bowling is fine. Madden NFL Football is fine. Candy Crush Saga is fine.

- No games until all the homework is done and all the chores are done.

The real challenge for parents comes in enforcing these guidelines. Some parents won't even try. Parents say to me, "I just want him to be happy. Playing Fortnite makes him happy. So why shouldn't I let him play?" But "I just want him to be happy" is a low bar. You can do better. Your son can do better. No child is born wanting to be a great scientist, or composer, or teacher, or entrepreneur. They must learn something of the scope of human possibility beyond what they see in a cartoon video game like Fortnite. In other words, it is your job, as the parent, to educate desire: to instill a longing for something better, more lasting, than video games...' [26]

Parents, please remember that your child does not have the insight to see games taking over his/her life. The changing brain of an adolescent makes them particularly susceptible to gaming addiction. You have to parent. It may strain your relationship at the start of enforcing limits, but it won't break that bond. In the long-term, it will lead to a better relationship. Discuss and invite your child to be a part of a problem-solving agreement over gaming.

The use of the word 'and' instead of 'but' when disciplining is more likely to invite co-operation. 'I know you want to keep playing, AND your time has ended. You can turn it off now, or it goes away.' You have respectfully validated their feelings and given them control over the situation and what will happen. Keep it short and straightforward. If they object, just give them a reminder that 'we had an agreement,' and if they turn it off, say 'Thank you for co-operating.' Make sure you follow through. If you don't, you will keep the problem going. You will be solving the problem for them instead of with them.

With a younger child, the word 'and' works just as well. 'I know you want to finish your game, and it's bedtime. Do you want one long story or two short stories at bedtime today?' You have given your child validation, control, and choice, which makes it more likely that you will elicit co-operation.

Pornography

The other issue that more often affects boys is pornography. Young children can easily stumble onto pornography while doing homework. They can mistype a search term in Google or click a link that eventually leads to a porn site. They are also using the internet to learn about sex and relationships, which is another gateway to porn. I remember watching a BBC documentary many years ago and being shocked that it suggested the average age for exposure to porn is 11.

The BBC's current affairs program Panorama obtained information and figures from 30 UK police forces, which reported that incidents of children abusing other children rose 71% between 2013 and 2017, and sexual offenses by children 10-years-old and younger have more than doubled since 2014.[27] Easy access to online pornography is listed as a strong factor behind these growing numbers. Of overall visitors to porn sites, 1 in 10 is under 10-years-old.[28]

ChildLine, a UK helpline and counseling service for under 19s, reported that 10% of 12- to 13-year-olds fear they have a pornography addiction. Two huge reasons for this are theorized to be the desensitization of children and the easy access to a mobile/cell phone.[29]

Pornography is also ravaging our Muslim communities. I have heard of cases where Muslim parents accept their sons watching porn because at least they are not dating! I am personally aware of pornography addiction of local Islamic school students as well as some Muslim elementary school students being exposed to pornography by their peers at their Islamic school.

There is an online program called 'Purify Your Gaze' specifically for Muslims across the world suffering from sex and porn addiction and other sexually compulsive behaviors. Participants include those who are regular mosque attendees and even women. To understand the scale of the problem, they have helped more than 57,000 men and women since 2009.[30]

The founder of 'Purify Your Gaze,' Zeyad Ramadan, was asked why so many Muslims are involved in something explicitly forbidden by the teachings of our deen. His response speaks volumes: 'One of the problems is that there is a large void in our community to talk about sex and healthy sexuality. There isn't opportunity for young, developing teenagers to start learning about sexuality in a way that is safe. And due to their curiosity and the lack of proper place, they start going online.'[31]

It bears repeating: There is a large VOID in our community in talking about sex and healthy sexuality. Look at the results. It is up to parents to fill the void before porn does that. In Chapter 3, I will guide you on how to fill the void for all different ages.

THE DANGERS OF SOCIAL MEDIA

There is a positive side to social media, where we can open our minds and learn about injustice. The success of the Arab spring was in part due to social media. We can also support various charities, do online courses, learn amazing information and stay connected to our distant relatives. Unfortunately, there is also a negative and dark side to social media.

Parents should outline basic etiquette and safety around online behaviour for their children. This includes explaining grooming to your children and the importance of not sharing personal information about themselves. Predators are waiting to engage with children and send them explicit videos. Tell your children that you expect posts to be respectful and not embarrassing to anyone.

I reminded my sons that what you post reflects your values and character, so think carefully about how you want to present yourself to the world. Tell your children not to click on links or pop-ups and check with you about search phrases and words to use when doing homework online. Keep the computer in a public place. I also made sure that my sons knew it was never acceptable to illegally download music or movies from the internet. You lose credibility as a Muslim parent if you don't attach a value to honesty and integrity.

California based psychiatrist Ustadha Rania Awaad, and spiritual counselor Hosai Mojaddidi cover the topic of parenting in the age of social media in a YouTube presentation. The first issue they raise is the large amount of time children are glued to technology in various forms and the fact that they are stumbling upon pornography.

Awaad mentions that thousands of apps aim to get youths into porn through backdoor channels, luring kids in using logos. Marketing is entirely intentional. The porn industry targets children hoping they become lifelong adult customers. They will use cartoon characters, free teaser images, and pop-up ads to entice children.

The issues with some apps are that they hide within other apps so your child can hide her/his nudes from you. Apps can also facilitate cyberbullying, promote hooking up, expose kids to profanity and explicit sexual content, and allow conversations between minors and predators to occur. Hooking up, being physically intimate with someone while not being romantically involved, is becoming acceptable. Children may be sent explicit videos and asked to imitate them and send it back resulting in sextortion. Online grooming where older men pretend to be teens has had some sad and even fatal consequences.

Get to know what apps are popular and what is on your child's phone. They are not all that they seem! Awaad states that with older teens, the most popular apps are WhatsApp, Instagram, Snapchat, Twitter, Vine, Tumblr, Pheed, Kik, and Ask.fm while 8- to 11- year-olds enjoy YouTube, Facebook, Moshe Monsters, and Club Penguin. Do you know about all of these apps? TikTok is currently very popular with kids as well as predators. Check out the 'useful resources' section at the back of the book about apps.

Mojaddidi recommends that parents regularly check their child's phone without warning, so they don't have time to delete things.

There are apps and monitoring software like Net Nanny that you should install on your child's phone to limit the amount of time they spend on a particular site or app. Thirty minutes a day is more than enough time allowed before being locked out. This will help them develop the habit of not wasting hours a day on Instagram or whatever app they like.

Awaad advises that parents use software controls as a starting point. 'You can't be disengaged, thinking oh, I'm not into technology. You can't afford not to know. You must stay current with trends. You need to follow your children on Facebook or Instagram.' She concludes by stating that we must seek refuge in Allah from every evil. This evil is growing. Are we taking spiritual precautions to protect our children?

The other issue with social media according to Awaad is that it is creating kids who need constant validation at an early age. They take loads of photos before they decide on the 'right' one to filter then post. This selfie generation is exacerbating self-absorption and narcissistic behavior. The fact that Kim Kardashian had a bestseller book called Selfish, which contained all her selfies, speaks volumes about this disturbing cultural phenomenon.

Awaad asks the question, 'Are you trying to be a friend to your child, which can cause you to become too relaxed with the rules?'[32]

Prophet Muhammad (PBUH) advised us to play with our children up to the age of 7; discipline and teach them between 7 and 14 years, then befriend them from 14 to 21 years of age. What does this look like? Your relationship should have some characteristics of friendship such as warmth, affection, enjoying time together on a consistent basis, vulnerability, talking, and active listening. However, you have to remember that you are not their friend, you are their loving, strict but fair parent.

THE SCHOOL ENVIRONMENT

You are not with your children all the time, and there comes a time when you cannot control everything that they do. They spend up to 7 hours each day at school, surrounded by values that don't align with yours. Peer pressure and bullying can make school life miserable. Even teachers are not necessarily always good role models. Instead of modeling acceptable language, I was disappointed to hear a teacher telling kids 'Don't piss off any teachers today,' when they were leaving his classroom in the morning. The level of disrespect shown by some Grade 7, 8 and 9 students towards adults is disappointing. I've experienced equally disrespectful behavior in an Islamic school.

Basic manners are greatly lacking. I've even had to remind youths to say please and thank you! Manners are essential in Islam and must be explicitly taught and modeled from a young age. I made sure my sons were always aware of the need to greet the elders in a gathering first as well as to thank a host after being in their home. These behaviors became second nature, which were positively reinforced by adults commenting on my sons' politeness.

Peer Pressure and Challenges

When I was growing up, I experienced a lot of bullying. But at least every day when I went home, there was a respite from it all. Nowadays, with social media, cyberbullying, anonymous trolling and peer pressure can be relentlessly 24/7.

Peer pressure at school and social media have seen the rise of various challenges. The need to belong and fit in is strong enough to make kids take part in things that are dangerous and pointless. The Ice Bucket Challenge that went viral a few years ago at least raised money for ALS (Amyotrophic

Lateral Sclerosis, also known as Lou Gehrig's disease, or Motor Neuron Disease). I have seen Grade 7 kids take part in the Eraser Challenge, where they rub the skin on their arms fast and hard with an eraser, and then compare wounds. These may be in the form of abrasions, burns, and even possible infections. An online drink challenge encouraged teens to make themselves a drink with as many edible but ridiculous ingredients as possible. They may have felt sick afterward, but they thought they were part of a new trend. There is currently a game being played by junior high girls called Scorpion where one student will dig her nails between the thumb and forefinger of another girl until she says scorpion.

Mental Health Challenges

Mental health issues such as anxiety, depression and self-harm are on the rise for youths. It is not surprising, considering the pressure on teenagers to conform, look cool, have trendy clothes and shoes, get good grades, be popular on social media and in school, be an extrovert, navigate complex hierarchies in social friendship groups and have a list of activities, experiences, and volunteer work for their resume.

When I was teaching in the UK, almost half of the girls in the class I last taught had issues with self-esteem, anxiety, eating disorders, depression, and self-harm. I've seen this get worse over the last few years. There is a lot of pressure on youths and young people to be extroverts. Our society doesn't value introversion or those who sit in lessons in quiet reflection. You must have something to say. I had to comment on their communication skills for university references, and those quiet, reflective students were always at a disadvantage despite their other strengths. What message does this send out to young people? That you are not good enough if you aren't 'out there' with a big personality?

Social media has contributed to this rise in mental health challenges because we look at filtered versions of other people's lives on Facebook or Instagram, which can lead to feelings of loneliness, stress, inadequacy, and depression. Social media also enables cyberbullying which can continue the bullying at school. There have been a few cases recently of children at elementary school who died by suicide due to bullying. Even at junior high/middle school, I have seen students voice suicidal thoughts.

Dangers of Drugs

Beyond social media, drugs are also an issue for the youth, including those who are Muslim. I have seen junior high kids getting expelled for marijuana use as well as for bringing in LEAN drinks to school. There are different names for this drink, including dirty Sprite, purple lean, and sizzurp. Pre-teens, teens, and college/university students make this drink by mixing three ingredients: prescription-strength cough medicine containing the opioid codeine, soft drinks such as Sprite, and flavored candy. This drink is addictive and impairs motor functioning. Teens can quickly lose track of how much they are drinking because this drink tastes like candy. I am personally aware of Muslim youth and young adults being a part of the LEAN scene and suffering opioid addiction here in my local community. This is also affecting other Muslim communities abroad. A BBC documentary called Hometown: A Killing explored the growing problem of Pakistani Muslim youths who are drug dealers.

Taking drugs is not something that only 'bad' kids do. Many youths can succumb to curiosity and peer pressure, and it can take just one moment of indulgence to become addicted to drugs. My younger son has never missed a day of fasting and is mindful of his prayers, yet he succumbed to his curiosity by trying weed once while on holiday in Amsterdam. He told me once was enough and I told him I was glad because our body is a trust from Allah. My older son has a friend, a practicing Muslim, who regularly smokes weed. Yes, Muslim kids that attend the masjid are also experimenting with drugs. Research in 2010 found that American Muslim illicit drug use was 25%, similar to the American non-Muslim population.[33]

Drug addiction is a health issue, not a criminal issue. We need to humanize those addicted to drugs, and be mindful of the language we use, avoiding terms such as 'potheads' and 'crackheads.' Nobody chooses to become addicted to drugs. We must talk about drugs to our children, so they know about addiction as well as the other hidden dangers of drugs being laced with fentanyl or other dangerous substances including 'softer' drugs being laced with 'harder', more addictive drugs.

Alcohol

Drinking culture is huge in senior high school and university. The pressure to not drink is too hard for some Muslims to cope with. My sons told me about some Muslims they knew who started university as non-drinkers but couldn't sustain their abstinence, and before long were consuming alcohol. There is little current research about this issue. The last study done in the USA in 2010 cites that 47% of Muslim college students drank alcohol in the previous year, of which 70% had done so before starting college. Even though 26% of the Muslim students felt religion was important, they still drank alcohol.[34]

MUSLIM-SPECIFIC CHALLENGES

Islamophobia

The biggest challenge our Muslim youths will experience is Islamophobia. I can remember a couple of incidents my son experienced. He was in Year 9 and was asked to go and meet with an Ofsted (Office of the Standards of Education) inspector. Upon leaving the classroom, one of his peers said, 'They must have found where you planted the bomb.' He was also asked, 'Is Osama Bin Laden your dad?'

These comments represent the post 9/11 world that our children growing up in the West are in. These challenges do need highlighting because they can cause isolation, depression, and alienation leading Muslim youths to disconnect from their communities. They are then at higher risk of joining in the haram activities of their non-Muslim peers.

There has been an increase in reports of children being bullied, teased and assaulted for being Muslim, mostly in school settings by other students and sometimes even teachers. The discrimination and feelings of rejection or alienation from the school environment may lead students to suffer from low self-esteem, which adversely impacts their physical and mental health and also their grades.[35]

The Yaqeen Institute published research on the impacts of Islamophobia on youth in the West, and these were some of the results:

1. Internalized Racism, a phenomenon where you adopt the stereotypes you hear about yourself. 1 in 3 Muslim children between the ages of 5 and 9 didn't want to tell others they were Muslim; 1 in 2 didn't know whether they could be both Muslim and American, and 1 in 6 sometimes pretended not to be Muslim.

2. Identity confusion. Young people often feel that they must choose between being Muslim and being Western, which can lead to social isolation or even abandoning their Islamic values.[36]

I remember high schoolers talking about being forced to wear their traditional clothing instead of jeans and being embarrassed about it. They also mentioned the difficulty of having strict parents who didn't allow them to go to the mall with their friends. When this happens, kids start associating Islam with not being allowed to do anything fun.

We come from a tradition of respect for elders and authority, and yet youth are surrounded by a culture where parents and authority figures are disrespected, which causes cultural dissonance. Having a persona at home and a different one outside the house can be challenging, but many youths do have these dual identities. It is stressful to not have an integrated identity and can easily lead to the youth detaching from their culture. I recently attended a lecture at a masjid where the speaker, a specialist in youth development and empowerment, spoke of this dual identity causing huge mental health issues for Muslim youth.

The Yaqeen Institute report on Islamophobia concluded that proactive support from parents is needed to keep Muslim youths secure in their faith and identity in these extremely challenging times. The Qur'an has also instructed parents to do this. 'Protect yourselves and your families from a Fire whose fuel is people and stones' (66:6).

Meeting a Marriage Partner

The other challenge our Muslim young people face is meeting someone for the purposes of marriage. Our kids are socializing and going to school/ university five days a week with non-Muslims of the opposite gender, yet we make all efforts to keep our Muslim boys and girls apart.

A Muslim boy once asked me, 'If I grow up knowing only non-Muslim girls, why do my parents expect me to marry a Muslim one?' Many Muslim communities conduct community events and activities in a gender-segregated way. Young people are not given any chance to observe and model gender interaction that maintains religious principles. We expect our young people to keep their values, yet we make it difficult for them to meet their desire for intimacy by not facilitating interactions for marriage. These young people have reported that holding on to their values is difficult, given the peer pressure; sexualized pop culture; and the natural desire for a physical and emotional relationship.[37] As a Muslim community, we need to make it easier for our young people to get to know each other.

Extreme segregation has also led to extreme behavior. The practice in Afghanistan of dancing boys, Bacha Baz, is an example. In this country where women are confined mostly to their homes and completely covered, boys dressing up as women and dancing for men to earn money is common. The primarily adolescent boys are then taken home by older men and sodomized, a practice that is culturally sanctioned.

After reading through the challenges of raising a Muslim child in the West, it can make you feel helpless and possibly cause you to lose hope. Take comfort in the reminder that our children are a blessing to us, but they are also a test. '...your children may be but a trial: but in the presence of Allah, is the highest reward' (Qur'an 64:15). You are going to be tested by your children but doing your best to guide them will ultimately yield rewards. Revisit and return your 'rules' about gaming/social media/TV/music to remaining God-conscious. This will help your children both spiritually as well as keep them safe from the dangers of this world.

The theory of Positive Youth Development, or PYD states that we need to identify protective factors that promote healthy development and reduce risky behavior. One of the most significant protective factors cited for our children is their relationship with their parents and families.[38] Work on staying connected to your child's daily life. I discuss this connection in the next chapter.

CONNECTION

I only get to the issue of talking about sex with your child in the last chapter of this book. There is a reason for this. Our lives are all about connection and relationships, which are the building blocks for healthy sex and sexuality. If your children are older and you wish you had connected better earlier, commit to improving this connection and start now. The formation and maintenance of this connection will strengthen the parent-child relationship, which is a protective factor in reducing risky behavior.

All human beings need and seek connection. We are born to share our life experiences. If children don't feel a connection at home, they will find it elsewhere. If you can help your children maintain a relationship with Allah, learn to love themselves, and remain connected within the family unit, you will be helping them build the strong, healthy foundations that are needed for them to become dependable spouses and parents.

PARENTING STYLES

Different parenting styles are going to foster connections in different ways, so parents should reflect on this. A style too authoritarian or strict where you may say things such as 'you will do as I say,' 'end of the discussion,' or 'because I said so,' is always going to be a recipe for rebellion. I've seen situations where parents are too strict, and their kids opt to attend university as far away as possible. There is a possibility that your child will embrace the good and bad of this newfound freedom. Rebelling is about going against that controlled upbringing and doing 'whatever I want.'

The other extreme is laissez-faire or permissive parenting, characterized by few boundaries, too much freedom, and a lack of discipline.

The middle ground between these two, authoritative parenting, is the best style for children's healthy development. These parents listen to the opinions of their children, consider their feelings, and allow them some role in problem-solving and decision making. Parents use positive and loving discipline and consequences instead of being unduly punitive and demanding obedience. They are teaching their children to develop a sense of inner discipline to regulate their behavior, which builds confident children with healthy self-esteem. Authoritative guidance is an excellent way to prevent harmful mainstream culture from being adopted. These parents have clear expectations, rules, and boundaries and hold their children accountable for their behavior. They do not rely on bribery and treats to get good behaviour.

We often hear that you will parent in the same style as your own upbringing, which shows how influential our parents are. My mother and father would have been considered lawnmower parents because they tried to make life easy for my siblings and myself by removing obstacles. They struggled with implementing boundaries, curfews, chores, and with saying no to us. The desire to do things for us came from a place of good intentions, love, and kindness because both my parents had difficult and stressful lives growing up.

I made the same mistake of becoming a lawnmower/helicopter parent for some time. I didn't want my sons to experience discomfort, so I 'did' too many things for them. I made excuses that they had homework and did the dishes for them. I would pick them up when they could easily have walked home. I even did homework assignments for them a couple of times so they wouldn't get in trouble with their teachers instead of letting them face those consequences. Thank God their father, my ex-husband, didn't do this and created a counterbalance to my parenting. I did work hard on becoming more conscious of my parenting in order to move away from this tendency.

The principles of attachment parenting and positive discipline have always appealed to me. A lot of the parenting workshops and courses I attended adhere to the Adlerian tenets of parenting. In a nutshell, parenting revolves around the idea that children want to belong and feel significant and that a child that misbehaves is a discouraged child. Misbehaviour is down to an unmet need. Discipline is firm and kind and focuses on solutions instead of being punitive. No physical punishment, such as spanking, is used because the outcome is that children learn to obey only to avoid punishment. Spanking doesn't teach them the inner discipline needed to behave better. Having two sons, I knew that one day they would be bigger and taller than me. I didn't want them to ever learn that physically hitting someone is okay in any circumstance. Allah also encourages this behavior. In chapter 5, verse 8, the Qur'an says, '...be just; that is nearer to righteousness....'

The practice of Prophet Muhammad (PBUH) was one of treating children with kindness, affection, and gentleness. Warmth and love are fundamentally crucial to the self-esteem of children, and our Prophet (PBUH) was generous in providing children with both. Let this be our model, even when we must correct behavior.

Usama bin Zaid narrated: 'Allah's Messenger used to put me on (one of) his thighs and put Al-Ḥasan bin 'Ali on his other thigh, and then embrace us and say, "O Allah! Please be Merciful to them as I am merciful to them"' (Sahih al-Bukhari, vol. 8, 32). Hugging and physical touch are so crucial to our development that cuddle cafés have popped up in cities for those who do not experience any physical contact. Do a Google search and you will find both physical and psychological benefits to hugs and cuddles. Prophet Muhammad (PBUH) knew this 1400 years ago.

We should embody attributes that are characteristic of Allah. Therefore, we should be merciful, forgiving, just, kind, grateful, loving, compassionate, and patient towards our children because '...Allah is with the patient' (Qur'an 2:154).

Parenting is a tough job. It requires endless amounts of patience, kindness, firmness, and love. Some days, all of those are in short supply. We must remind ourselves that we will make mistakes, and we will mess up. We may ignore our children when they want to connect or yell at them over something small. We may overindulge them because we feel as though we are not spending enough time with them. We may use the TV as a babysitter too often. Sometimes, we may not even like our children. Parenting requires sacrifice, patience, and perseverance, and there are no shortcuts. Human beings are not perfect, but our ideal role model is Prophet Muhammad (PBUH), and Islam is about striving. Each day we should seek Allah's help and try to do better.

The right parenting strategies will strengthen your relationship with your child, enabling you to hold more influence. Home life will be more peaceful as well, but ultimately, it's about more than that: you are moulding the foundation that shapes their values and character to help them stay on the right path. You must establish the supremacy of the parent-child relationship over the relationships with same-age peers. A good book to help with this is *Hold on to Your Kids: Why Parents Need to Matter More Than Peers* by Gordon Neufeld and Gabor Maté.

CONNECTION TO ALLAH

The starting point of connection to Allah should be based on love rather than fear. It will be easier for your children to hold on to their faith through the difficult teen years if they feel connected to Allah and wish to please Him. This will make them less likely to go astray.

Make sure you are always improving your Islamic knowledge so that you can instill in your children the following traits: ikhlas (sincerity); akhlaq (good character); adab (manners and behavior); taqwa (God-consciousness); tahara (physical purity); and tazkiya (purity of heart). According to Abu Hurairah, Prophet Muhammad (SAW) said: 'Allah makes the way to Jannah easy for he who treads the path in search of knowledge' (Muslim, Book 13, hadith 6).

How do you instil this connection?

Focus on the wonder of creation. Go outside for a walk and point out the beauty of nature: the chirping of the birds; the building of a nest; the importance of the work bees do; the symmetry in a butterfly's wings; and the different smells and colors of flowers. I am fortunate to live near the Rocky Mountains in Canada, and every time I visit, I am in awe of our Creator. Children have different temperaments, and this includes their spiritual temperament, so you must find different ways to build their connection to Allah. Prayer is essential but be sure to nurture a love of the outdoors as well, as another form of connecting. Whenever a snowfall happened, I would take my sons outside to enjoy the snow. Sometimes we would come in and watch a YouTube video about the intricacies of a snowflake, again marveling at Allah's creation.

Talk about the blessings in your lives so that you can establish salah as a way of saying thank you to Allah. By shifting the mindset like this, salah will become less of a burden and you will instill a love of Allah. Needing to perform a prayer to thank Allah is very different from praying because 'if I don't, I will go to hell.' Also teach your children why prayer is important. Allah doesn't need our prayer, we need it. We must fear Allah, but a relationship based primarily on love is more likely to endure. Saying 'Let's go and thank Allah for keeping us healthy and for having good food today,' may mean we won't have to push them to pray.

Don't miss opportunities to talk about Allah. Even just picking up a piece of litter is telling your child that we must keep Allah's planet clean. This attitude will also instill feelings of gratitude, for Allah tells us in the Qur'an 'If you are grateful, verily I will increase you (in it)' (14:7). There are many benefits to developing a mindset of gratitude. Gratitude helps remove social comparisons and therefore makes us happier. It allows us to feel better about ourselves, which strengthens our trust in Allah. We want our children to always find peace in our Creator because '...In the remembrance of God do hearts find satisfaction' (Qur'an 13:28).

Read stories regularly about all the prophets, peace and blessings be upon them, to show your children their faith and the obstacles they endured. Stories captivate children and in Surah Yusuf, it states that 'We do relate unto thee The most beautiful of stories...' (Qur'an 12:3).

Teach your children about the Names and Attributes of Allah, and that we have a special place amongst creation. Use Allah's names in your du'a such as Al-Mahaymun (the Protector). Read about the companions who became firm believers and good role models. There are many contemporary Muslim authors publishing fiction books for children, so as your children get older, explore these also.

There are always opportunities to link everyday conversations to Allah and Islam. My son once commented on how much money the rapper 50 Cent made in a year. Here was an opportunity to discuss how this may look like success because lots of money means you have 'made it' in the Dunya. Do we want to be winners in the Dunya or in the Akhirah? Discuss religion with your teens instead of just lecturing them which can cause them to tune out.

Help your children get to know the Qur'an. There is a Hadith that states that 'The most beloved actions to Allah are those that are consistent, even if it is small' (Sunan an-Nasa'i, Vol. 1, Book 9, Hadith 763). They are many English translations available, including a version for children, making the Qur'an more accessible than ever. Connect them to the community through camps, halaqas, youth groups, picnics, and other events so they grow up being comfortable as part of the Muslim community. Try to live near a masjid so it is easily and regularly accessible. Feeling connected to Allah and Islam is essential to counteract the internalized Islamophobia children are being poisoned with. Youths have had an important role in Islam and must not be sidelined. Prophet Muhammad (PBUH) gave the youth roles and responsibilities, whether in battle, saving his life, or teaching Islam. In Surah Al-Kahf, the sleepers of the cave were young men. Youths were engaged, empowered, contributing members of the community. If we want our youths to follow this example, then we should be building their self-esteem and resilience from a young age.

Both parents should be actively involved in instilling Islam into their children. Living your values is something that should be role-modeled for children. Teach by example. The most significant gift my parents gave us is a strong sense of social justice and kindness. Having grown up in South Africa under apartheid, my father used to return to the townships and run free health clinics and deliver free diapers and clothing, including our Eid clothes and shoes. He lived those values of social justice and compassion. He spoke up when Muslim shopkeepers tried to overcharge African clients. My mother was also involved in fundraising and charitable endeavours. You need to live the life you want your children to live, and my parents have passed that legacy down to me and my siblings. Connect your children with serving others and link that to Islam. Let them see you serving others, whether by buying a homeless person something to eat or volunteering at the food bank. By doing so, you are helping to present Islam positively and foster kind behaviour. My son and I slept rough to raise money for homeless youth some years ago. We slept on a cardboard box in the Nottingham UK city center/downtown for a night. Although it was spring, by the evening, it was cold and uncomfortable. In the morning, we were fortunate enough to be able to go home to warmth and food, where so many others couldn't. This experience was also a way of shaping my son's character by developing his empathy and the principle of always looking at those less fortunate instead of envying those who have more. My children also joined me in a protest when Israel attacked Gaza. I've tried to live my values, so my sons understand that we stand up for injustice. We also did bag packing at a grocery store alongside youth with disabilities because I wanted them to learn empathy and gratitude for their abilities. Their piano teacher was an older man who lived on his own and barely cooked. I used to invite him to have dinner with us, which again gave my sons a lesson in empathy and compassion. These acts impacted my sons in positive ways. They noticed the child in class who didn't get a Christmas card and would give them one the next day. If we passed a homeless person, they would ask if we could buy them some food. They would talk to the child with special needs that was sitting alone. Develop kind children by being kind. I used to remind my sons that we need to be striving every day to do good deeds, so they outweigh the bad ones on our scales. 'So whosoever does a good deed equal to the weight of an atom will see (their reward). And whosoever does a bad deed equal to the weight of an atom will see (their punishment)' (Qur'an 99:7-8). Since my sons were raised seeing these behaviors around them, they, too, will do the same with their children, in shaa Allah.

Parents, make verbal remembrance of Allah a part of your everyday life, so that your children are regularly exposed to the concept of putting trust in Allah and seeking His help and His pleasure daily. It helps to remind our children that constant sinning will rust and seal our hearts from Allah's guidance. 'Verily there is rust on their hearts from what they used to do' (Qur'an 83:14). 'Allah put a seal over their hearts and on their hearing, and on their sight is a veil' (Qur'an 2:7).

My sons were 1- and 3-years-old when my mother died. They came to the cemetery when she was being buried. My three-year-old threw dirt into her grave. I never kept my sons away from going to the cemetery when someone died. Visiting a cemetery is always a strong reminder that we will all end up there and that death is a part of life. It made talking about death less scary for my sons because they also learned that we must strive to be good so that one day we can see those family members again. As they got into their teen years, I used to say that our words and actions will either make our Qabr light and spacious or dark and tight. It was a good reminder of accountability to Allah. Children's innate fitrah is to worship Allah; it just needs to be nurtured and reinforced daily.

CONNECTION WITH THE SELF

The second part of the connection between you and your child is building up their self-esteem and self-love. There are significant challenges about identity that young Muslim youths are facing. We need to be raising confident teenagers who have high self-esteem. Take advantage of youth camps and youth groups, which will provide your children with Muslim friends who share similar values and provide them a support system. Yes, Muslim kids aren't always 'good' kids, but your children may be a positive influence on them and vice versa.

There is a saying that tells parents to give their children roots and wings. Give them a solid foundation based on Islam and also allow them to soar. By giving them wings, you are allowing your children to take risks; develop problem-solving skills; form and offer their opinions; and make choices. Providing these opportunities will help your kids feel competent and capable, which leads to self-confidence.

When we become helicopter or lawnmower parents, we are trying to make life comfortable for our children. The intention is good, but children also need to experience some occasional discomfort in order to learn from it. By allowing this experience, you are gifting them with the belief that they are capable, resilient and able to survive life's ups and downs. Spoil your children with hugs, love and compliments but don't always do things for them that they can do for themselves, for it makes children believe that others should do everything for them. It also minimizes the consequences of their choices. This is taking away accountability and responsibility, and those are what build self-esteem.

We sometimes do things for our children that they can do themselves because it may be quicker and easier, but in the long-term, we deny them an opportunity to learn 'I am capable.' Don't make their bed in the morning or do the dishes when it's their turn. Instead of tying your child's shoelaces when he/she wants to have a go, teach him/her one or two steps at a time and let him/her learn. You are allowing them to feel capable.

How to Build your Child's Self-esteem
Allow some risk-taking

I remember watching a documentary which mentioned that not allowing your children to take risks while growing up results in them being more likely to choose unhealthy risks when they are older. Supporting children in stepping outside their comfort zone opens them up to new opportunities and helps their self-esteem.

My siblings and I grew up with an overprotective father. We were pampered to the point that the principal of our school had to drive us home when it rained so that we wouldn't get wet. Being capable is also learning to take responsibility for your actions. My parents would write a note to teachers to say I was sick if I overslept or wanted to get out of the gymnastics class at school. They didn't want me to get in trouble and wanted me to be happy. My parents were kind, generous people who tried their best, but any parent will always have room for improvement.

Growing up, I took few physical risks because of being overprotected. I wasn't allowed to climb trees out of fear that I could fall and break a leg. My dad was a GP (general practitioner) who sometimes worked in the Emergency Department of a hospital, so he saw a lot of injuries, and this caused him to be protective. He intended to keep me safe from harm. This came from a place of love, but it also had a cost. How could I become confident in climbing a tree if not given any opportunity? When I was 10-years-old, I wanted to participate in a charity walk called 'Miles for Millions,' which later became 'Metres for Millions' when Canada went metric. You get people to sponsor you with money for every mile you walk.

But my dad didn't allow me to do the walk because I could get blisters. It was too far, and I hadn't 'trained' for it. My dad didn't want me to be hungry, thirsty, tired, hot, and possibly have blisters on my feet. Good intentions, but the messages I heard as a child weren't positive. All I heard was that I won't be able to climb the tree; I will fall. I won't be able to learn how to climb a tree; it's too hard. I won't be able to walk for a long time; I will get blisters. I can't do it; it's too hard if I haven't 'trained.' All these messages revolve around not being capable and competent, even though it would have never been my parents' intention to make me feel that way. 'I can't' became the little voice in my head that reminded me I was not capable and competent. Imagine if I had been allowed to take a risk and learned how to climb a tree. Perhaps as an adult, I would have taken up rock climbing because I would have seen it as an acquirable skill. Instead, I became cautious with everything I did because I was always scared of getting hurt. I can recall telling my father I wanted to pursue a career in business and him saying 'business is a man's world.' My father was trying to protect me from what he thought was a dog-eat-dog world and directed me to a different way to serve people. So, I studied nursing, which I ended up leaving because I didn't like it. In the end, not allowing some risk-taking can limit your child's potential to believe in themselves and to choose their own career path. I was always guided to play it safe as a child, and this affected me negatively in the long run.

Establish routines

Routines are essential to give children a sense of comfort and security, two ingredients that are necessary to make them feel confident. Routines also help them understand time; establish habits, such as brushing teeth; and provide a focus for 'together time.' Add on extra time to your schedule so your child can be involved in routines such as folding laundry or making up beds. Toddlers and preschoolers love to help (pity it doesn't always last!); it makes them feel a sense of accomplishment and builds their self-confidence.

Give your children chores

If children get into the habit of doing chores when they are younger, this behavior becomes a part of healthy family life. They learn that everybody needs to work together to keep a household running. Even toddlers can put clothes into a washing machine, building their competence and self-confidence. Doing chores from a young age teaches skills that will help children become independent one day. Many sites list age-appropriate tasks for children. You can use the list below as a guide or to help give you some ideas:

Ages 2 and 3

Personal chores

- Assist in making their beds
- Pick up playthings with your supervision

Family chores

- Take their dirty laundry to the laundry basket
- Fill a pet's water and food bowls (with supervision)
- Help a parent clean up spills and dirt
- Dust
- Stir something for baking
- Get them a kid-sized broom to sweep
- Push buttons on the washer or dishwasher
- Carry in an item of groceries

Ages 4 and 5

Note: this age can be trained to use a family chore chart.

Personal chores

- Get dressed in minimal parental help
- Make their bed with minimal parental help
- Bring their things from the car to the house
- Pick up their toys
- Wash hands

Family chores

- Set the table with supervision
- Clear the table with supervision
- Help a parent prepare food
- Help a parent carry in the lighter groceries

- Sort colours for the laundry
- Match socks after clothing is washed
- Answer the phone with parental assistance
- Be responsible for a pet's food and water bowl
- Dust with supervision
- Hang up towels in the bathroom
- Clean their room with supervision
- Clean floors with a dry mop

Ages 6 and 7

Note: this age can be supervised to use a family chore chart.

Personal chores

- Make their bed every day
- Brush teeth
- Comb hair
- Choose the day's outfit and get dressed
- Write thank you notes with supervision

Family chores

- Be responsible for a pet's food, water and exercise
- Vacuum individual rooms
- Wet mop individual rooms
- Dust individual rooms
- Fold laundry with supervision
- Put their laundry in their drawers and closets
- Put away dishes from the dishwasher
- Help prepare food with supervision
- Clean their room when asked
- Empty indoor trash cans
- Answer the phone with supervision

Ages 8 to 11

Note: this age benefits from using a family chore chart.

Personal chores

- Take care of personal hygiene
- Keep bedroom clean
- Be responsible for homework
- Be responsible for belongings
- Write thank you notes for gifts
- Wake up using an alarm clock

Family chores

- Wash dishes
- Wash the family car with supervision
- Prepare a few easy meals on their own
- Clean the bathroom with supervision
- Rake leaves
- Learn to use the washer and dryer
- Put all the laundry away with supervision
- Take the trash can to the curb for pick up
- Test smoke alarms once a month with supervision
- Screen phone calls using caller ID and answer when appropriate

Ages 12 and 13

Personal chores

- Take care of personal hygiene, belongings and homework
- Write invitations and thank you notes
- Set their alarm clock
- Maintain personal items, such as recharging batteries
- Change bed sheets
- Keep their rooms tidy and do a biannual deep cleaning

Family chores

- Change light bulbs
- Change the vacuum bag
- Dust, vacuum, clean bathrooms and do dishes
- Clean mirrors
- Mow the lawn with supervision
- Prepare an occasional family meal

Ages 14 and 15

Personal chores

- Responsible for all personal chores for ages 12 and 13
- Responsible for library card and books

Family chores

- Do assigned housework without prompting
- Do yard work as needed
- Babysit
- Prepare food - from making a grocery list and buying the items (with supervision) to serving a meal – occasionally
- Wash windows with supervision

Ages 16 to 18

Personal chores

- Responsible for all personal chores for ages 14 and 15
- Responsible to earn spending money
- Responsible for purchasing their own clothes
- Responsible for maintaining any car they drive (e.g. gas, oil changes, tire pressure, etc.)

Family chores

- Do housework as needed
- Do yard work as needed
- Prepare family meals - from making a grocery list to serving the meal – as needed

- Deep cleaning of household appliances, such as defrosting the freezer, as needed

From the article "Age-Appropriate Chores," © 2009, 2016 by Focus on the Family. Originally published at FocusOnTheFamily.com. Reprinted with permission.[39]

It is so vital for us parents to empower our youth, which in turn increases their self-esteem, building their confidence in their Muslim identity. Many Muslim parents do not foster independence or critical thinking, denying their children the practice of learning to make decisions and become independent.

My sons both moved away to different cities for university when they were 18 years of age and had to become independent very quickly. My younger son lived with a couple of Pakistani boys in his first year of university. He commented that they couldn't cook a single dish and didn't know how to do laundry. We must teach our children these skills to foster independence and competence. This starts when they are young with such tasks as tidying up toys; choosing an outfit; and going to find an item in a different aisle when grocery shopping; as well as experiences like spending a night away at grandparents; walking to the corner store; walking home from school; helping prepare a meal; taking the city bus; and so on. However, with young children, don't push independence on them if their temperament and comfort needs still require dependence.

Give them some control and choice

Giving your child a choice can start with clothing, and it doesn't matter if their outfit doesn't match. Kids who always feel controlled and feel like they have no say will rebel sooner or later. Giving them a choice allows your child to be part of the decision-making process, which makes them feel valued and respected. At the start of an activity or visit to someone's home for a playdate, I used to tell my sons, 'I will let you know when you have 10 minutes, and then 5 minutes left.' By doing this, I allowed them some control over how to spend their last 10 minutes, and they were aware that the end was coming.

Encourage a hobby or develop a skill besides video games

Kids are most likely to give up on an activity, hobby or sport between the ages of 12- and 14-years-old. Try to help them develop an interest in an activity before they get to that age and encourage them to hold onto it. It will give them something to keep themselves busy with as well as increase their competence, confidence, and feelings of accomplishment if they stick with it. It will also help them discover their strengths and abilities.

My younger son had to be supported into activities so I would always stay until he felt comfortable enough for me to leave. It was the only way he would try anything and that was okay. When my sons were 6 and 8 years of age, they took up badminton and took it to a competitive level that they kept up through their teens and onto university. The exercise kept them fit, and they learned the skills of sportsmanship and how to be a team player. They also had to learn the discipline of maintaining their schoolwork alongside a passionate hobby. We added music lessons so that they could have a creative outlet. We always offered them a choice, but I felt it was essential to get them into something enjoyable and beneficial, which kept them away from the gaming culture. It was a balancing act because I didn't want to overschedule them either. There is much research around today that cites the necessity of giving children downtime, without technology, where they can be bored to stimulate their creativity and imagination. Boredom facilitates attachment to the family. We don't always have to be filling up their free time with play dates. I used to take my children camping in the summer, where no phones were brought along (except for mine), and it was just the outdoors and free play.

Let them experience failure

Failure allows us to experience different emotions—anger, sadness, and frustration, for example—which are vital for our development. We want to raise emotionally intelligent children. We want them to be okay with understanding and expressing their feelings; they will need that skill to build a future relationship. Failure is a part of life, and it gives children a chance to reflect on their mistakes and consider how they can improve. It also fosters a growth mindset where failure is seen as an opportunity to grow.

Always winning never gives a child the chance to learn to lose gracefully and to appreciate the value of effort even when it doesn't result in success. Sharing your own mistakes and how you learned from them is quite valuable. Your children will be watching how you handle making mistakes. Do you chastise yourself? Or do you acknowledge that we all make mistakes, and that's okay?

Failure also allows us to see our strengths and our weaknesses realistically and helps us develop perseverance. Reframe both success and failure in an Islamic way. Their successes and failures do not define them; their character does. Our success is a blessing from Allah, and our failures are a way to get closer to Allah and ask for his help. When my son didn't achieve the grades needed for entry into medicine, I explained that this was also a blessing. My son could now do a foundational pre-medicine year before starting medical school. He was a summer-born child, so he was always one of the youngest at school. This extra year gave him a chance to mature and start medical school the following year. My son graduated from medical school in the top 10 for overall grades. I told him that this was a gift from Allah to be used to help others. Raising self-esteem must be balanced with teaching humility, which leads to gratitude and contentment. Humility is an important Islamic trait, as mentioned in the Hadith, 'Verily, Allah has revealed to me that you must be humble towards one another so that no one oppresses another or boasts to another' (Sahih Muslim 2865).

Praise, don't overpraise, and encourage

Don't wrap your child in so much cotton wool that all they ever hear is praise or overpraise. Be kind in words—don't humiliate your child—but be careful with overpraising. They can sense when you are lying. If I had told my son that he was the best badminton player on the team, he could have started thinking that he was or always must be perfect, which would have put a lot of pressure on him. If everything your child does is 'incredible,' they will stop believing in the sincerity of your praise, rendering it meaningless. Children should learn that it takes time and practice to become competent at things.

Don't use general comments like 'good job', but rather praise specific effort and progress. Perhaps something like, 'Your hard training worked for you in this game. Your skills as a goalie have gotten better.' This lets them know you are paying attention and giving them ownership of that result, which is how you healthily encourage your child.

Provide support

Don't ever make them feel as though they are a disappointment. Encourage and let your child know that you have faith that they will make better choices next time or that they can get through a difficult time. When my son was incredibly disappointed with some exam results, I said, 'I know you are disappointed with your grades, but I have faith that you will know if you need to look at how you're studying before your next exam.' I offered further support by saying, 'Do you want to get some help in looking at your studying strategies which could help you to study more effectively?' He needed some time to be alone, so I just left him to ponder on it. A couple of days later, he took up my suggestion and decided to meet with a teacher to improve his study skills.

Ask them for their opinion

Your children need to start to develop and defend their beliefs; a useful skill for when they must answer questions about Islam. Even if they express a conclusion that does not align with yours, which may disappoint you, keep the conversation going in a non-judgmental way. If children feel as though they can express themselves without being condemned, they will be more likely to speak up in the future. Asking them what they think is also attaching value to what they have to say, making them feel respected and boosting their self-esteem. You are becoming the askable adult by keeping the door open and ensuring they will come and talk to you.

My younger son enjoys purposely expressing an opinion opposite to mine because he thinks it's funny and likes to see where the conversation will lead. It can be frustrating, but I've learned to think of it as him developing his critical thinking skills in providing a counterargument to my opinion.

Don't let them compare themselves to others

Tell your children they will never win this fight. There will always be someone better at something, or taller, or slimmer, and so on. Also, do not compare them to their siblings, relatives, and friends. You may be thinking that you are motivating your child by comparing them to someone better, but instead, you may foster jealousy or cause self-doubt and even erode their relationship with you because they don't feel accepted as they are.

Tell them to work on being the best version of themselves, not the most popular person. We have to fight against the notion that it is necessary to be popular and get our children to understand that. We don't want our children to depend on appearance, popularity and grades to define how they think and feel about themselves. We all have different strengths, so don't put all the focus on their academic success. Celebrate your child's individuality. Your child may discover they have a lot of patience when babysitting, have a talent for drawing, are a natural comedian or are mindful of reading Qur'an.

Use daily affirmations

Remind them that they are a unique and original creation of Allah. Have your child pick a different affirmation each week to repeat to themselves every day. It may be 'I am kind,' 'I am enough,' 'I am hardworking,' 'I am caring,' or 'I make people happy.' The more they say it, the more they will believe it. Also, be sincere in answering questions. For example, if your child says, 'I'm ugly,' don't say, 'Don't be silly, you are beautiful.' They are not going to feel beautiful just because you've said they are. You haven't listened to your child and validated their feelings. The message they receive is that they can't tell you how they feel because you will belittle their feelings. You are indirectly saying that they shouldn't feel those feelings, and this will shut down communication. It is better to say, 'Right now, you are saying unkind things to yourself. I'm sorry you feel that way. Let's talk about what makes you feel that way and what will help you to feel better about yourself.' A follow-up conversation can be held about not letting the words of others impact them. The word 'ugly' is meant to take power away from an individual.

Children must also get affirmations from you. Tell them they are worthy because of their kindness, generosity, humor, creativity, and so on. Remind them that Allah created them to be remarkable. Catch them doing good things, so they can hear positive words from you.

Build your child's resilience

Building the self-esteem of our children is also about building their resilience to withstand negative comments or labels and not letting such negativity define them. It is essential for children to develop resilience early because the rate of mental health issues peaks in adolescence. Building resilience is about empowering our children.

We all want to raise children that can cope with life's ups and downs without crumbling. Part of this is teaching children that having their feelings is okay, but they must also learn how to deal with them. Be accepting of their feelings. If your child's pet dies, 'It's only a hamster, you can get a new one' doesn't validate their feelings. 'Don't make a big deal out of it,' 'Stop behaving like a baby,' and 'How can you be hungry, you just ate' are all statements that do not acknowledge feelings. Try instead, 'I can see that you are angry/upset/hurt that your brother broke your toy,' followed by, 'but you can't hit him. You can hit a pillow or draw a picture of your angry feelings.' With hunger, say something like, 'If you still feel hungry, what healthy snack would you like?' With the pet scenario, consider saying, 'I know you miss Fudge (hamster). He was lucky to have you looking after him.' By using these statements, you will have respected your child's feelings, allowed them to own those feelings, and shown them that they can cope with this disappointment.

Get involved with your child's school life

By getting involved, you will remove the feelings of 'us' and 'them' that likely exist in this environment. Regularly participating in events or becoming part of the PTA helps non-Muslims see us positively and will make it easier to do things like go in with Eid treats, give a talk on Ramadan, and talk about school issues. In this way, you will also model getting involved in your local community and school life to your child. By creating a sense of belonging to their school community, you will aid their growing self-esteem. Support them in their studies throughout their schooling life.

Support them in widening their social circle

Develop relationships with family and friends. Let your children be a part of social engagements which will teach them to be socially competent. Don't let them sit in the corner playing on their phones. Your children are going to strengthen ties of kinship, which are essential in Islam, and gain a supportive network through these relationships. They will learn what kinds of qualities they like and respect in others.

CONNECTION WITH FAMILY

It is essential to build love and respect within the family. A good connection to the family will be the foundation of support your child will need to make good choices. Is there a good atmosphere in the home? What do your children observe between their parents? Do they see the affection and respectful conversation? Do they see how to apologize and ask for forgiveness? How are you resolving conflict: with a shouting match and silent treatment, or with compromise and negotiation? You are modeling their perception of a healthy relationship and what to bring to a marriage. Don't underestimate this power.

Do your children see your face light up when you see them at the end of their school day? Make your child feel like they matter and remind them that they are valuable and loved. Say 'I love you' often. Have a weekly ½ hr individual time allocated per child and a monthly date with a teen. Alone time helps you to check in, connect, and get to know them as individuals. What are their likes, dislikes, hopes, fears, dreams, and favorite things? This specific time is especially important following the birth of a sibling, which is a significant change for a child and can easily make them feel pushed out. By doing this, you are strengthening your relationship with your children, so they come to you first. If individual time is a new idea for your family, don't force bonding. Perhaps just suggest lunch, instead of 'we need to spend time together' which may invite resistance. We do know that kids like food so this will be an easy win.

Communication

How well do you communicate with your children? What are you doing to strengthen your communication with them?

Listen

Your listening skills are going to be in high demand in the teen years. Your teen will be more likely to listen to you if you acknowledge their feelings and listen to them. Teens don't like you problem-solving for them because it makes them feel judged. Through listening, you should be coaching them to come up with their solutions, as this makes them feel capable and therefore develops their resilience. Through this, they are learning that they can deal with a situation and find a solution themselves.

Make sure you are an active listener. That means putting the phone down and giving them some undivided attention if they are sharing something with you about school. They will see your support and will be more likely to keep talking to you when they are older. Stay calm when they speak to you about something untoward or adverse in their day. If you overreact, they will be less likely to talk to you again the next time something happens.

A great time to communicate with teens is in the car when you are sitting side by side. This setup is always less threatening. As the teenage years approach, adolescents are making sense of their own beliefs, so don't stop them or make them feel bad about questioning something.

Build excellent communication early, to ensure they talk to you about what's happening in their lives, and you can continue to hold some influence.

Conversation Tips and Great Questions

When I used to pick up my then 5-year-old son from kindergarten, he was always tired. The last thing he wanted to do was have a conversation. If I asked him, 'How was your morning?' I would get generic one-word answers like 'good' because, at that age, he hadn't built up sufficient expressive language skills. I reconnected with him with an 'I missed you, happy to see you' and share something about my day before he promptly fell asleep in the car.

Using open-ended questions is the best way to generate two-way communication because it requires more than a yes or no answer. Prompting your child develops these skills and is a way of building your connection to them. An example of an open question would be, 'What's the best/weirdest/funniest/hardest/kindest/ meanest thing that happened today at school?' Just remember that even older kids need time to decompress and don't like to be bombarded with questions as soon as you see them. Before bed can be a good time to have a conversation. There are helpful conversation starters in the 'Useful Resources' section of this book.

When your kids are helping you in the kitchen, ask questions like 'What's going on at school?' 'What are kids getting up to?' 'Are any kids dating?' 'What songs are most popular this week?' and 'How do you feel about the behavior of your peers?' As they get older, ask them questions like 'What kind of person are you looking for?' and 'What qualities will you avoid?'

Respectful language

Respect is a two-way street. Model and treat your children with respect so they see it and learn to embody it. If they are disrespectful, a 'you' statement like 'Don't/how dare you speak to me that way' or a command such as 'Go to your room,' creates defensiveness and anger, so stick to 'I' statements. 'I can see you are upset/angry/hurt. Do you want to talk about it?' Acknowledge how both of you are feeling and take some time out. 'You are upset/angry, and I would like to be spoken to with respect' or 'let's take 15 minutes away before we talk again' are good statements to use. You want to have a mutually beneficial solution instead of a punishment, which may make you feel in control but is often only a short-term solution. Two-way respectful communication removes the power struggle.

'Put that away now,' can become 'In 5 minutes, I will need you to finish that and put it away.' This slight change in tone makes it easier to gain co-operation. A timer will be useful for young children. For older children, instead of saying 'you need to clean your room,' which is a command and will create defensiveness because of the word 'you, try 'What about your room?' Parents often talk too much; sometimes one word, such as 'Room?' is all that's needed.

Always model respectful language when speaking to your child and those around them. Don't be above apologizing to them when you are wrong. If you have been overly authoritarian or permissive also offer your children an apology. 'I'm sorry if I get angry quickly/don't listen enough/ haven't helped you become independent enough/talked about topics I should have etc., but I'm trying to learn to do better.'

FAMILY TRADITIONS

We live in the most connected, yet also the most disconnected era. I remember waiting at the Toronto airport for an evening flight back to Edmonton. The waiting lounge was quiet because everyone was on their phones. Couples sitting beside each other, and even entire families sitting together, were all on their phones. I've seen it in restaurants, while people are walking, and even from mums pushing strollers. I watched a TED talk a couple of years ago that mentioned that the quality of the conversation goes down by 80% by having your phone on the dinner table. It is important for us adults to take note of how much time we are also spending on our screens if we are to limit our kids' screen use.

Our busy lives are causing disconnection. Dinner with the family sitting around the table is being replaced with kids eating in their bedrooms or everyone watching TV with dinner plates on their laps. We need to reconnect. A great way of unifying a family is traditions. What memories and traditions are you building?

Family traditions are a great way of connecting and stimulating bonding for a family. Traditions are as unique as a family is. They can include family jokes, annual vacations, or a yearly summer picnic. Other traditions could be shared hobbies, weekly family meetings, or designated family time like board game nights or dinner with the extended family every month. A monthly dinner alone with each child is a great way to make each child feel special. A giving back to the community initiative can also become a tradition. This could be something like helping at an Islamic food bank together, as a family. Traditions create comfort and security. We may have moved to a new house, or my parents may have divorced, but Friday night is still pizza and movie night. Don't let overscheduling get in the way of traditions. Slow down to grow relationships with your children. Keep it relaxed and enjoyable. Also share your family history with stories of obstacles and challenges that have been overcome as this will inspire resilience.

Eat Meals Together

Are you ensuring that the family sits down and eats meals together? Keep mealtime a phone-free zone so family members can learn to enjoy each other's company, check-in, and renew their connections. Keep the TV off during meals. Help build communication skills by encouraging everyone to talk about their day. Mealtime is also an excellent time to talk about family values and traditions. Studies show that kids whose families eat dinner together regularly experience better grades, more emotional stability, less depressive symptoms, less obesity, and fewer eating disorders.[40]

Family ties are significant in Islam, and traditions help to reinforce this. At Eid, we always had food favorites, like biryani. We watched Hawaii Five-O together as a family, and we ate our dinner together. We would go as a family to watch my father play cricket, soccer or run marathons. We had regular religious events at our home. We had a family restaurant we always went to for special occasions.

My late parents would always buy the crib of the first child born to my siblings and myself, and each grandchild got a quilted blanket made up of squares that my late mother made.

As an adult looking back, I've realized how important these traditions were to build unity and meaningful connection between members of our family. They provided a chance to reminisce about shared memories. I know people that live in the same city as their siblings and cousins and rarely see them. They often talk about missing that connection in their lives. All of them wish they had family traditions. Our traditions shape our family life and tell us things about our family, our history, and our values. Some family traditions connect us to our past. Visiting relatives throughout our lives is also a way of reconnecting with our birthplace.

There are many great ideas for establishing family traditions. See the 'Useful Resources' section if you need inspiration. The traditions that have been a part of my own family life are:

1. For Ramadan, we always had special savories for Iftaar. Making a Ramadan calendar and lanterns would be a good tradition for children.

2. For Eid, we always had a milky nut drink on Eid morning, and certain desserts and cookies were always baked.

3. When my sons were young, we would lay in bed on a weekend morning and watch Thunderbirds together.

4. We used to take regular family walks to disconnect from technology and connect with nature.

5. Bedtime stories were part of our nightly routine.

6. We used to play board games in the evening on weekends.

7. Sundays were always a traditional roast dinner.

8. We went to the same camping site around the same time in the summer.

9. We cooked a big breakfast on the weekend, which might be waffles, pancakes or eggs and sausages.

10. We had regular spring cleans to declutter and let someone else benefit and use what we didn't need.

11. When my sons were teens, I encouraged them to contribute to family life and learn a skill by making one meal per week.

12. My sons used to look forward to our monthly trip to a tea shop for toasted teacakes.

13. We did yearly charitable work where we gave our time which was something tangible for the children to learn gratitude, and how to help others instead of just donating money.

14. My niece has her daughter hold up a mini-blackboard stating what grade she is going into every September, which is something I love. It captures the change at the same time each year. They also go for a yearly family portrait at the same time each year.

15. Every New Year's Eve, my brother sets the table with name tags, menus, fine china, and silverware for the 5-course dinner that he prepares for his family.

What could you do to build a happy family life? There are entire books written on the topic. Remember to base your behaviour on building strong ties of kinship and kindness because 'Verily, the most complete of believers in faith are those with the best character and who are most kind to their families' (Sunan al-Tirmidhi 2612).

Eat at least one meal a day together and hold weekly, bi-weekly or monthly family meetings to consider which aspects of family life are going well and which need improving. Try to always resolve conflict before going to bed by having everyone bring a solution for consideration to the table and agreeing on it before anyone leaves.

In this chapter, I discussed three areas of connection. Here is a summary of the key points to remember:

A. Connection to Allah

- Focus on the wonder of creation
- Focus on being grateful
- Familiarity with the stories of the prophets, Allah's Names and Attributes, and Qur'an
- Serving others as a way of strengthening their idea of Islam
- Connect with the community through youth groups, halaqas, masjids, youth camps, iftars

B. Connection with self

- Build your child's self-esteem and resilience
- Allow some risk-taking
- Give them routines and chores
- Give them choices
- Help them develop hobbies, skills, and interests
- Allow them to make mistakes
- Use appropriate praise
- Ask them for their opinions
- Avoid comparisons
- Use daily affirmations

C. Connection with Family

- Strengthen your communication skills: talk about the smaller things regularly in daily life; use respectful language always
- Have regular family meetings
- Develop family traditions

You might be thinking 'what does this have to do with talking about sex to your children?' Strengthening your child's connection with Allah is developing their imaan. You want them to grow up feeling a great love for and loved by their Creator, so they remember they are answerable for their actions and don't cross the red line.

Developing their self-esteem is vital to giving them the confidence to be proudly Muslim, which will help insulate them against the peer pressure of drinking, drugs, and engaging in sex.

The family connection is meaningful because that's where values, beliefs, and morality are built. Children need to want to spend time with the family. Family time must be treasured so children grow up feeling safe, loved and accepted even if they make mistakes or poor choices. Don't let a child decide to forego a family holiday because their friend said they can stay with them. Family meetings and family dinner time are ideal times for conversations around sex and media to be happening. Family movie night can also be a place for teaching moments.

Ultimately, we want to shape the values and beliefs of our children in such a way that they are obedient to Allah and guard their sexuality. Make them feel loved and worthy so they don't go looking for love elsewhere until they are ready for marriage. Support them in developing the skills to resist peer pressure. Make du'a for strength and the commitment to do what you need to do in order to parent effectively.

This chapter was all about setting up the foundation to make conversations around sex easier. The next chapter will discuss how to have those conversations.

CHAPTER THREE

HOW AND WHEN TO TALK ABOUT SEX

As Muslims, we need to gain knowledge. As the Quran says, 'My Lord! Enrich me with knowledge' (20:114). Parenting should be instinctual, but it has become necessary to learn how to parent children raised in a digital world. Parenting is a lot more than just finding your child a good school and Qur'an class, making them healthy food, ensuring they get fresh air and exercise daily, and a nightly bedtime story. The context of the world our children are growing up in now requires conscious and intentional parenting. It is a lot easier to build up a good view of Islamic sexuality with young children than trying to piece together the broken ideals of a teen. You must teach your child to know and love their body enough to respect its value.

Islamic scholars and Imams advise us to talk to our children about sex and sexuality, but they don't tell us how to speak to them. This chapter is going to help you with that. Firstly, we have to change our mindset on talking about sex. We have to remind ourselves that this is something good from our Creator. We are explaining something natural and normal. You are not taking away your child's innocence, not talking to them will. You will feel uncomfortable—and that is okay—but if you start when you children are young, you will begin to create dialogue with them, and these conversations will get easier. Words such as erection, ejaculation, orgasm can be hard to say but these are normal and amazing functions that Allah has designed for a purpose. Consistent mini talks instead of long lectures should begin when children are young, in order to normalize talking about sex. Over time, the awkwardness will decrease. These conversations need to be revisited regularly which opens the door to further discussion. As you continuously build on previous information, your children are processing your values. One talk isn't enough to counteract all the many incorrect messages our children are getting from other sources.

Remember that no two children are alike. Some remain entirely innocent for a longer time and will be satisfied with just a bit of information, whereas other children will require a full explanation. If you need to say, 'I will tell you when I think you can understand it better,' then make sure you follow through with that. If your child is not satisfied with that response and wants an answer, then give them an answer. Do not brush them off. You don't want them to be left feeling as though it's not okay to talk about this subject. We are responding to the changing context of a world where according to the RCMP, 8-year-olds are sending nudes,[41] peer on peer sexual assaults are happening in primary schools[42] and porn is being accessed by 11-year-olds.

The most important thing to remember is that we are meant to be preparing our children for a loving marital healthy relationship, which has Allah's barakah in it. Our role as parents is to shape their character, values, and beliefs while giving them the skills and support to learn how to handle their sexuality in an Islamic way.

According to Islamic Network, an organization doing work with Muslim youth under 21 years of age, 'In 2018/19, the two most common areas of questions from both boys and girls were (1) LGBT related or about (2) explicit sexual practices.'[43]

I've saved this content for the last chapter of the book for a few reasons. You needed first to understand the challenges our children are facing so you can provide anticipatory guidance. Their connections to Allah, themselves, their parents, and their family will be their anchors against peer pressure and the media. As stated previously, you must strengthen the parent-child bond by making your children feel that they belong, that they matter, and that they are loved. This relationship between you and your child will help in positively influencing the choices they make, so I have given you tips to strengthen it. Now you must begin the task of bringing sex education into everyday conversation.

'The affair of the believer is amazing, for there is good for him in every matter...' (Sahih Muslim 2999). This means you have an opportunity to do good every day in this matter. Our children are a trust from Allah and guiding them is a form of dawah.

The societal message is that the right age for sex is when it feels right for you! Sex does not mean a commitment. We decide our morals as individuals. Our bodies are ours to do as we please. I listened to a Christian couple and loved their expression on the necessity of talking about sex to your children: 'God commands it; wisdom demands it.'[44] Some essential principles to guide you include those that follow.

START YOUNG

- You can progress gradually and regularly. If you try to suddenly enforce rules, this will cause conflict, especially in the teen years, when they are carving out their identity, and their peer group becomes significant.

- Islamic morals and values need time to develop. Start when they are young, so these morals and values get reinforced and strengthened as your child grows.

   For example, privacy and modesty are learned, so you need to teach your children to knock before they enter your bedroom. The Qur'an mentions that once your children reach the age of puberty, they should ask your permission before entering your bedroom (24:58). You should also knock before entering their bedrooms when they get older.

- Starting young lets your children know that they can come to you with any issues or problems.

- Your children will become used to open conversations, empowering them to be more comfortable sharing their thoughts and feelings, and keeping you in the loop of their daily lives.

If your children are older and you haven't had these conversations when they were younger, start now. You may feel a bit awkward doing it, but be honest and say: 'I'm feeling a bit awkward and nervous right now,' or even 'I'm embarrassed right now, and this is new for me, but I need us to start to talk about it.' Yes, your kids may think this is random or weird, but you need to do it. Being open lets them know that this is essential information that they need to hear.

   A good starting point for conversations is when you have some shared time together, whether in the car sitting side by side, which is always less threatening, or while having your weekend breakfast. Sometimes doing an enjoyable shared activity is also an excellent time to have conversations around sex with both your sons and your daughters.

REMOVE THE STIGMA

Children are not born with embarrassment or shame attached to sex; that comes from our behavior. Always using the proper names for body parts helps removes stigma and taboos. If you wait until they are teenagers, the discomfort is greater, and if it's the first time they hear you say the words vagina and penis, they are going to be thinking, 'You want to be telling me this now!' Besides that, their peers and porn have already gotten to them.

NO SHAMING

Allah has blessed children with curiosity and so they will wonder about their own private parts as well as those of a sibling or friend and may want to see what's 'down there,' so it's common for you to see them play doctor.

If they have not had any conversations around their body parts, then their natural curiosity will get the best of them. Do not shame them but do explain that 'our private parts are ones that are kept covered. Islam teaches us to be modest, which means keeping them covered and private.' Explain that 'Allah has made us into boys and girls, which means our bodies are different. We don't touch or look at someone else's private parts, and nobody should touch or look at yours. Allah made boys and girls different because we need each other, and we will grow up to have different roles.' My older son was 5 when he asked me, 'Do you have a *willy?' I explained that I was a woman, and no, I don't have a 'willy.' He asked me, 'Where do you pee from, and can I see it?' He followed me into the bathroom because he wanted to come and see. I told him that our private areas are those we keep covered so no, he can't see, but I have an opening for the pee to come out. He wanted to know what it looked like, so I drew him a picture.

*I, unfortunately, used the slang word 'willy' with my sons instead of penis, but I didn't know any better at the time. In my family home growing up, we also used nicknames. I've heard cupcake, fairy cake, pee-pee, wee-wee, dangly bits, and other similar terms used by parents to refer to genitalia.

Abu Umama Al-Bahily (may Allah be pleased with him) narrated that a young man came to the Prophet (PBUH) and said: 'O Messenger of Allah, give me permission to commit Zina.' The Companions turned to him and started rebuking him. The Prophet said, 'Come closer,' and asked him if he would like this for his mother, daughter, sisters, aunts, and so on, and he answered no to each of those. The Prophet then placed his hand on the young man and prayed for him, 'O Allah, forgive his sins, purify his heart, and protect his chastity.' This man wasn't shamed but rather empowered to not give in to his temptation.

Be mindful of your tone of voice and response, which can shame a child. Saying 'I can't believe you're asking me that,' 'You shouldn't be asking such things,' 'It's not appropriate,' 'Why do you want to know,' or completely dismissing the question can stop them from asking you further questions. Avoid making such remarks to avoid completely losing your influence.

BE HONEST

When I was growing up, we used to hear that if you engaged in masturbation, you could go insane or cross-eyed. Kids need facts; being dishonest erodes trust. If a child sees you not praying because you are on your period, don't say it is because you aren't well. You will confuse them if they then see you cooking or carrying on with daily life. If ever a question catches you off guard and you don't know what to say, do not be afraid to say 'I'm glad you've asked me that question but I just need a little time to think about how best to answer you. Let me get back to you,' and do so. Thank your child for coming to you with the question.

TALK ABOUT RELATIONSHIPS

Pop culture seems preoccupied with your sexual status. Have you done it or not? It is less concerned about the building of a mutually satisfying and caring sexual relationship. Young people are not being prepared to learn how to love someone else. Sexual education in schools focuses mostly on puberty, contraception, STIs and pregnancy, and less on relationships. Parents should be filling in what is lacking in the classroom and should refocus on building relationship skills.

As your children grow, your conversations should become primarily about relationships and not just the mechanics of sex. Relationships are fundamental at every stage of our lives and are the key to a happy life.

Start teaching your toddlers and preschoolers about boundaries and consent. Seek permission to tickle your child and stop if they don't like it. Teach your children that they can say no to kisses, hugs, and sitting on laps. If someone takes offense, then be your child's advocate and say, 'I'm teaching Khadija to be aware of her feelings and speak up for herself, so please don't take it as rudeness.'

School-age children can be asked about friendships and loving relationships. 'What makes somebody a good friend?' or 'How do Mum and Dad show you they love you?' You are teaching them about qualities in friendships such as someone having your back, listening to you, and being kind. All these characteristics help them build their moral compass.

Adolescents need to be talked to about mutual respect and consent as part of a healthy relationship.

Boys need information about relationships as much as girls do, and they are often stereotyped as only thinking about sex, which is entirely untrue. The high school boys I spoke to had questions about relationships such as 'How do you let a girl know you like her?' and 'What if she doesn't like you back?' Boys are not used to being as open with their feelings as girls because of societal conditioning. There is also apparently '… an epidemic of young Muslim men who don't know how to talk about love, and don't realize how badly they'll need to.'[45]

Therefore, boys need more emotional nurturing to become comfortable talking about their feelings, a necessary skill for a healthy relationship. From infancy, build up your son's emotional vocabulary to avoid stereotyping of roles and to nurture their emotional development. Let them play with dolls and get them a pet to learn 'nurturing' skills. They don't have to conform to gender stereotypes. If your son wants to learn how to knit, let him. Read them books where male characters ask for help or show vulnerability and express their feelings. Empower boys by listening and allowing them to depend on us. Don't tell your sons 'big boys don't cry' or shame them when crying by minimizing the issue as something trivial. Be affectionate and cuddle them as often as you would your daughters. My best friend's husband used to call their sons 'sunshine' from a young age. While boys are referred to as 'slugs,' 'snails,' and 'puppy dogs' tails' in nursery rhymes, I thought 'sunshine' was such a great word for boys to be called. I followed their lead and call my sons 'sweetness' to this day.

The underlying principle which should underpin your conversations is presenting sex as a gift from Allah to a married couple. Keep your messages positive because that is more impactful. Sex is the ultimate act of intimacy that two people can share. The message our children need to get is that sex is a sacred act because it is so special. We also want our children to see this as an act of worship that should be pleasing to Allah, which it will be if saved for marriage. Islam has a positive view of sex; it is not only for procreation. Clear explanations of sexuality need to include the virtue of chastity, as well as its challenges. We need to demystify sex, so it isn't a taboo subject and so that you, the parent, can be the primary source of information for your child. Knowledge is the only way to empower your child to make the right choice.

BE AN ASKABLE ADULT

As mentioned earlier, the Muslim youth want to talk to parents, even though mum and dad aren't talking! You are their role model, through your words and your behavior, and are their most important source of information. Become ask-able, so that your child is comfortable coming to you and knows they will be listened to and respected. Ideally, dads should talk to their sons and moms can talk to their daughters about sex but there can also be overlap about topics like relationships and pornography. It will be helpful for your sons to know about things from a female point of view and daughters from a male viewpoint. If dads aren't willing to do their part and talk to their sons, then find a willing relative or mentor to do so. Alternatively, mothers can step in and do so. I know a few Muslim mothers who had to talk to their sons about sex because their husbands wouldn't.

TEACHABLE MOMENTS

It's not possible to tell you what to say to a child at every age, but many everyday situations can become teachable moments that start a conversation. These moments can create the ideal conditions to ask questions, make a comment or act as an icebreaker. Teachable moments allow for short snippets of dialogue instead of a lecture. Some examples include:

- seeing an actress in a bathing suit;
- the pregnancy of a family member, friend, neighbor;
- changing a diaper;
- seeing a breastfeeding mother;
- seeing a kissing scene;
- TV shows/movies/songs/ads/magazines which show gender stereotyping, sexualized images, LGBTQ issues, dating, and sex;
- ads for sanitary products, tampons, and condoms;
- going to a wedding; and
- news stories, such as the #MeToo movement.

Ask your child what they think. These are excellent times to explain your beliefs and values.

TALK AND LISTEN

Listen to what your children are asking, so that you can answer appropriately. 'Where did I come from?' may not be a question about sex but rather geography! Give your child time to absorb information without overwhelming them. You can try to find out what they already know or have heard and use it to give them the correct information. Don't be afraid to use books as a starting point for answers. You don't have to know it all.

*If your child asks a question about sex in front of relatives, don't ignore or shush your child, but rather take them aside and say something like 'I'd like us to sit down, just me and you, so I can answer that question for you.' If you can't respond immediately, then perhaps something like, 'I don't have time right now, but later we can talk.'

Teens

Teens require more forethought because they will withdraw and start using their friends as a source of information. You want to keep the communication going because your teen is changing. Puberty is happening along with changing moods, testing boundaries, and wanting independence. This is a critical age for them to learn that other people's values are going to be different from ours as Muslims, though you should expect these values to be challenged. Your teen is trying to assert their own identity, which is a typical developmental task.

When you talk and listen to your teen, treat them like a mature person as this kind of treatment makes them feel as though their views and feelings are respected even if you don't agree with them. Accept that they will make mistakes and do things that you won't always approve of and let them feel safe to admit mistakes. Make sure that they feel your unconditional love.

MODEL A HEALTHY, AFFECTIONATE, AND RESPECTFUL RELATIONSHIP

I recently heard Mufti Menk give a talk where he said that kids need to see their parents be affectionate towards each other. You are meant to be modeling a healthy relationship. Be aware of how you handle conflict as a couple because your children are watching. Is there a respectful compromise? Do they ever see their dad washing dishes or helping with other household chores as our Prophet (PBUH) did? We should be striving to raise a generation of boys that can clean, cook a meal, and do laundry. You are helping your son be a better husband and fostering a better relationship with your future daughter-in-law, who will thank you. Be aware of your cultural biases. What messages are you sending to your children? Do you fall into the trap of taking responsibility for childcare all the time because you are a woman? Do you ask your husband if he can 'babysit' his own children? Do you have different expectations and rules for your sons and daughters?

These general principles will be helpful in guiding you, but it is also useful for you to be familiar with the stages of sexual development so you can understand what to expect and how to deal with it.

SEXUAL DEVELOPMENT NEEDS OF CHILDREN

The information below on sexual development and how to support your child is based on the site used by Alberta teachers for sexual health education in schools. A more comprehensive and detailed outline and a parent guide can be found on www.teachingsexualhealth.ca [46]

Birth to Two Years

- Babies explore their bodies and have an increased awareness of the bodies of others.
- They receive messages about trust and love through physical touch and holding.
- With diaper changes, boys will, at some point, begin to grab their penis because they are exploring their whole body, which is perfectly normal.

How to Support your Child

Your toddler needs to learn that their body is special, exclusive and private, so you must use the correct names for genitals, such as vulva (outer female genitalia), vagina, and penis. Using the correct terminology not only removes the taboo and shame associated with our genitals but also enables children to communicate information in case of abuse. Telling a teacher 'my uncle touched my 'cupcake' means little, but 'my uncle touched my vagina' can help stop abuse that's occurring.

Tips for Strengthening the Parent-Child Bond

Attachment – The developmental task for the first year of life is attachment and trust. The only way a baby can let you know they have an unmet need is through crying. If your baby is not responded to, they feel that their world is not safe and reliable, which erodes their trust. They can then grow up to be a clingy toddler and may have difficulty with relationships throughout their life.

There is also pressure on parents to get their young toddlers started on playdates and exposed to lots of children. They do not need this. They don't learn social skills from being around kids their own age. Strong caregiving and adult attachments are where they will learn these skills. There is nothing wrong in cultivating friendships, but they don't need lots of socializing in the early years.

Connection before correction-This should be the foundation for discipline for all ages. You need to connect with your child before you can correct their behavior. When children are upset/angry/crying/anxious, their brain is in fight or flight mode and you cannot reason with them. If you are too angry to deal with your child, count to 10, remove yourself for a short spell, and then deal with them. Remaining connected to them means not isolating them but staying physically close and reassuring them while you deal with their misbehavior in a tone that remains warm and not threatening. Parenting is ultimately about building a relationship with your child. You will be able to parent most effectively through connection. A strong connection means you aren't competing with their peers. When I was teaching, we were encouraged to correct work using the hamburger model: Say something positive at the beginning and ending and do the correcting in the middle. The same principle can be used when correcting behaviour. Starting positive increases the chances of a child listening before you begin the work of correcting their misbehaviour. Ending on a positive note makes the child feel unconditional love and that you believe in their ability to behave better.

Temper tantrums- Every parent will dread the start of temper tantrums, which are developmentally appropriate around the age of two. It is tough for a child to not have the verbal skills to deal with how they are feeling. Let your child explore what they are feeling and acknowledge it by saying something like, 'I know you are upset because you wanted to stay/want that toy.' We want to raise emotionally intelligent children who are not afraid to express their feelings, which is crucial when building relationships. Stay close to them. Try hugging them or ask them to hug you. This new focus can sometimes bring a child out of a tantrum entirely and keeps you connected to your child.

Sharing - Do not expect a toddler to share. They are not developmentally ready to do this. It is like asking someone to borrow their most prized possession. Put away favorite toys that will cause an issue if a playmate is coming over.

Distraction and Redirection - Keep them safe. Use a firm 'no' if they are going to do something which harms them or others. Otherwise, most misbehavior of toddlers can be managed with distraction and redirection to an alternative activity or place.

No labels - 'You're naughty,' and 'you're bad,' are labels which will become self-fulfilling prophecies. Even saying 'she's shy' can limit your child's potential because she will take on that label and believe herself to be shy. To avoid this, label the behavior, not the child. Instead of 'You're a good boy,' say, 'It was really helpful when you put your toys away.' You should not assign them traits at such a young age. Interestingly, I heard some research being spoken about on a radio show which found that it is a good thing to assign traits to older kids and teens. Comments such as 'you are not a cheater' and 'you are kind' actually promoted honesty and kindness.

Positive language - Say 'Walk' instead of 'Don't run' or say, 'Crayons are for paper, not walls.' Negative words like 'don't' are often not understood or taken in properly by young children. Older kids can easily tune you out and already go into argument mode, setting up a power struggle before you've even finished your sentence.

Respect - When you need to blow your toddler's nose, model respect of personal space and body by telling them beforehand. I have seen mothers' swipe in to wipe faces and noses without warning. Model respectful behavior and language in your interactions with your children and with those around them.

Prevention -Tiredness and hunger are common triggers for misbehavior. Try not to take your child out for a grocery trip or any other outing when they are tired and hungry. Sometimes misconduct can be prevented simply by taking their necessary comfort into consideration.

Preschoolers 3-5 years

- They may like the feeling of touching their genitals.
- The exploration of body parts continues, and you may see this manifest as playing doctor.
- A sense of gender identity begins to form.

How to Support your Child

As mentioned previously, they need to hear the correct names for their genitals—vulva, vagina, and penis—to normalize this language, promote a healthy body image and give them the speech they need to express what's happened if abuse has occurred. Reinforce the idea that there is 'safe touch' and 'unsafe touch.'

Preschoolers need to learn boundaries around nudity. I remember being at the Eiffel Tower with my children, and it was a scorching day. Some children, who looked up to the age of six years, were running into the fountain naked. In Islam, we teach modesty at a young age. Tell your child that Allah has made our bodies special, so we keep them covered. If your child likes to touch their genitals, gently explain that 'touching our private parts is not something we do in public. It is done in the bathroom or in a bedroom.' They don't need an Islamic explanation of haram and halal at this age, as it can cause shame. Teaching privacy is another concept that preschoolers can learn best when modeled, so they should see you knock if the bathroom door is closed.

Preschoolers must understand that no one can touch their genitals, and they need to tell you if someone does. Explain that sometimes a doctor or nurse may have to, but they will explain why. Sexual abuse can start at this age and your children must have an awareness of inappropriate touch in order to keep them safe. Sexual abuse happens to 1 in 5 children, and in order to combat this, the European Council has come up with the Underwear Rule, which is simple enough for a child to understand. No one should touch you on the parts of your body covered by your underwear. This is an 'unsafe touch.' This is a clearly defined boundary and you are teaching them to recognize danger.[47] Also teach your children assertiveness, 'I don't like that; please stop.'

Our religious values are not enough of a protection for our children. In the Muslim community, children are taught to respect adults. In some cultures, they may address them as Aunty or Uncle. The trust of parents can be won over, making it easy for a family member or friend to take advantage of and abuse a child. Most abusers are known to their victims and this is happening in our communities. There have been cases in the last few years of Imams molesting children while teaching them in Qur'an classes.

Tips for Strengthening the Parent-Child Bond

<u>**Islamic identity**</u> – The building of an Islamic environment in the home should start at the preschool stage. You should be laying the foundations of their Islamic identity. Up to the age of 7 years, we are to play with our child, but there is plenty you can do at home to develop their spiritual connection to Allah. Teach them short surahs and songs, let them hear Qur'an in the house, and allow them to participate in prayers. They won't sit still or follow through yet, but by being a part of these actions daily, you create a routine.

I don't advocate sending 4- and 5-year-olds to attend Qur'an classes. If they're just going to be hearing a story and songs for a short time without any formal learning, that would be okay, and that's all they need. Concentration for a child is their age plus two, so a four-year-old can concentrate for no longer than 6 minutes. I took my children out of their Qur'an class because the lesson was far too long and, in the end, they didn't like going. Their experience of learning about Islam was not likely to be positive if it didn't meet their developmental needs. Not all Qur'an teachers or those teaching Islamic studies have experience of working with children or know enough about their developmental needs to teach them effectively.

<u>**Rethink time out**</u> – I used time outs for both my sons. Recently I came across an article discussing how ineffective a time out is, and when I read it, I agreed. Having a child sit alone and reflect on their misbehavior is not effective. We should connect with them instead of isolating them, which creates feelings of anger and defiance. Talking maintains comfort and connection, making it easier for our kids to learn limits and respectful communication. We are not giving in to misbehavior but are connecting to correct it.

Punishment is a short-term solution to mischief that creates disconnection. Children will do what you want to avoid punishment, which is not a long-term solution. You want your children to develop inner self-discipline and an internal locus of control in order to be able to behave better. I spoke to my sons about their experiences of time-out when they were older and could think about it. They told me all they felt sitting there was anger towards their father or me. And in truth, it didn't work with them in terms of stopping the misbehavior it was meant to correct.

Five to Six Years

- They're amused by bathroom humor.
- The 'where do babies come from?' questions may appear.
- An increased shyness about their body develops and they will want more privacy.
- Their *gender identity is developing.
- They will continue the exploration of their own body.
- They may consider sexual words 'bad.'

*Gender identity has become a hot topic over the past few years, with some parents now raising children 'genderless' or 'gender-neutral.' Our gender is part of our identity, and we are born male or female. Nowadays, some clothing is unisex, make-up for men is available, it is trendy to give a girl a boy's name such as 'Scottie,' and gender and sexual orientation are considered fluid.

This topic also generates controversy because the number of children transitioning has been steadily increasing over the years. In response, a coalition of whistleblowers, academics, and medical experts in the UK have come together to release a forthcoming book to express their fears that teens are being wrongly diagnosed. The book also challenges much transgender ideology, which they feel psychologists are scared to question, and addresses the fact that GPs fear being branded transphobic.[48] Whether the book will generate conversation or controversy remains to be seen.

This book cannot do justice to the complexities of the issues around gender identity, and if you have concerns about your child in this area, I advise that you seek the advice of professionals and scholars. I also highly recommend the book *Why Gender Matters* by Leonard Sax, which covers this topic in detail.

How to Support your Child

As Muslim parents, we should affirm our child's gender and encourage their identification with the same-sex parent to strengthen that identity and feel comfortable in it. Both parents must also be affectionate towards their children. We can't change Islam to accept homosexuality or same-sex marriage, but our children should see us model Islamic values of respect, compassion, and tolerance towards those with a different sexual orientation or gender identity than ourselves. We live in an inclusive society, and we have Muslims that identify on the LGBTQ spectrum.

The two questions that seem to be universal amongst children of this age group are, 'Where do babies come from?' and 'How does the baby come out?'

Q: Where do babies come from?

At this age, they need short and simple answers such as 'Allah puts love between a husband and wife. When they want to share that love and are ready to look after a baby, Allah blesses them with a baby who grows inside the Mummy's womb.'

Q: How does the baby come out?

'Allah gave every part of our body a job. The private parts of girls and mummies have an opening called the vagina. When you grow up, and your body can hold a baby inside it, that opening can stretch and get big enough to allow a baby to come out when it's ready to be born.'

You should be adding the proper words such as bladder, urethra, urine, and stool to their vocabulary. Also explain that girls have two other openings, one for urine and one for feces and teach your girls about wiping from front to back and using water to clean themselves.

School-Aged Children 6-8 years

- You should expect this age to continue enjoying bathroom humor and to consider sexual terms as bad words.

- Same-sex attachments are important at this age.

- Gender identity is strengthened at this age, and there may be reverse role-play occurring such as a girl acting as the husband while role playing family life.

- Body exploration is common at this age, and masturbation can occur.

- More privacy is often requested as they become more embarrassed about their bodies. They may ask questions about babies and birth and are aware of reproduction.

How to Support your Child

For this age, continue using proper terms and be careful to promote a healthy body image because comparisons can start even at this young age. Don't let your children see you obsess over your appearance or weight. The sexualization of children's clothing becomes apparent at this age, so be mindful of the messages they are receiving. Pay attention to what they are wearing. I remember a Muslim friend of mine dressing her 6-year-old twin girls in long summer dresses and longer shorts with T-shirts instead of tank tops. She didn't allow crop tops, bikinis, or halter tops and short skirts so that it wouldn't be strange for them to not be allowed to wear these clothes when they hit puberty. Instead, she wanted them to learn modesty at a young age.

On the flip side of that, some parents may feel that while their daughter is still young, she should be allowed to wear whatever fashion is trending. If this is the case, as she gets older, explain that Allah has made different rules for what we can wear when we grow up. To make this transition more manageable, you must build your daughter's sense of self early on, so that she doesn't define herself by how she looks or what she wears.

Inappropriate Touch/Sexual Abuse

Conversations need to be revisited so, again, reiterate information about inappropriate touch. Make sure your children can assert themselves if someone tries to touch them by having a practice run of them saying, 'No, stop doing that.' Make sure they know that 'secrets' are not allowed, and they need to come and tell you if something has happened. I read an article recently on not encouraging children to keep secrets. Perhaps you tell them about their sibling's birthday present but say, 'keep it a secret.' We shouldn't use the word 'secret' but rather say 'keep it a surprise.' Groomers will often tell a child, 'This is our secret.' We cannot leave this to chance. Remember, most instances of assault happen with people we know.

Tell your child: 'It can be confusing when the person that touches your private parts is a family member or friend that has cared about you. They may even ask you to touch their private parts. They can do it in a gentle way and tell you it is something special between the two of you. This can make it hard to understand that it is wrong. If this happens to you, it is never your fault. The person doing this may be a kid, teenager or grown-up and they know it is wrong. They are taking advantage of you. They will tell you not to tell anyone. Tell someone you trust right away. Most people don't like talking about it, but you will feel better if you do.'

There should be parental controls on the computer, and they should be taught skills in internet safety, though they shouldn't be using a computer or laptop without supervision.

My sons did not have internet access on their phones until their late teens. If you are allowing internet access on your children's phones, then get yourself educated about apps, have parental controls in place, and check their phones regularly.

Q: Where do babies come from?

Start with reading the story of Noah's Ark and explain that 'Allah created everything in pairs. Day and night. Heaven and Hell. Male and female. Boy and girl. Allah made mummy and daddy different so they can make a baby together. Allah tells us to get married first before we have babies because He thinks that's what's best for a family. Inside Dad is one part needed for a baby, which is a very tiny cell called a sperm. Inside Mum is the other part, which is a tiny cell called an egg. When they join together, a baby will grow, and that is how you got started. You were once just a tiny seed. The Qur'an tells us so when it states "...We created you from dust, then from a small seed, then from a clot, then from a lump of flesh..."' (22:5).

In school, intercourse is explained in Grade 5, at about 10 years of age. Some children will need that explanation earlier than this because they're curious and want an answer. Look at the next section for an example of an explanation which you can use or adapt.

Q: How will it come out?

'Girls and women have two openings in their private parts. One is for urine (pee) to come out, and the other opening, the vagina, is like a tube that stretches till it's big enough for the baby to be pushed out. Allah has made our bodies very special to be able to do something so amazing.'

An animated version of childbirth will be helpful. Watch it yourself first and decide whether you would want to use it for your child and find it appropriate. The one recommended by Mamanushka, the site of two Muslimah bloggers, is good. It has over 27 million views and has a beautiful quote at the end: 'Pregnancy is a process that invites you to surrender to the unseen power behind all life.'[49]

Tips for Strengthening the Parent-Child Bond

<u>**Connection before correction**</u> -Instead of yelling, keep calm to reduce power struggles, but ensure you maintain firm and kind discipline. The Qur'an sets out the correct Islamic behavior, stating that we should be among '...those who restrain their anger and pardon men...' (3:133) and as reported by Anas Ibn Malik, the Prophet (PBUH) said: 'Calmness is from Allah, and recklessness is from Satan' (Al-Sunan al-Kubrá 18651).

<u>**Islam in the home**</u> - From a young age, raise your children to see Islam's presence in the house. Make Eid a big deal; exchange gifts, decorate your home, do a Ramadan calendar (there are lots of online resources for this), or Ramadan crafts. Your children must see Islamic values in your behavior. Getting your child to lie about their age to get into a movie or some other paid event at a lower price is dishonest. You are their role model, so behave as one.

Put in the work to strengthen their faith in their elementary years before adolescence starts, as this is when they will naturally pull away from you. You should be modeling behaviors that demonstrate kindness, co-operation, and empathy in all relationships as well as modeling an appropriate way to deal with conflict. Kindness is an important Islamic trait to nurture. Encourage kindness by asking your children 'what did you do today that was kind?' As Aisha reported: The Messenger of Allah, peace, and blessings be upon him, said: 'Verily, Allah is kind, and he loves kindness. He rewards for kindness what is not granted for harshness, and he does not reward anything else like it' (Sahih Muslim 2593).

Self-esteem – Friendships can be fickle at this age, causing your child's self-esteem to fluctuate, so they need careful nurturing to combat this. Catch them when they are doing things right and praise them. Create a sense of responsibility through chores to make them feel capable. Keep communication going and let them know you accept them for who they are.

Routines – A routine is still necessary for school-aged children. You can write down everything that needs to be done and work through it together. When they accomplish something, they feel capable and competent. My older son was always very slow to get ready in the morning. We had to write out a morning routine that gave him some independence and gave me some peace of mind because I wouldn't have to be nagging him. This invited co-operation.

SCHOOL CURRICULUM

By Grade 4, when children are 9-years-old, sexual education is introduced into the school curriculum in Alberta. This introduction causes anxiety and fear in many Muslim parents, and it shouldn't.

Recently in the UK, Muslim parents wanted to drop from the curriculum the 'No Outsiders' program, which promotes LGBT equality and challenges homophobia in primary schools. Four-hundred parents in a predominantly Muslim school pulled their Muslim children out of school in protest of this program. The school responded that the LGBT community is spoken about in a small number of lessons, in the context that differences are fine and with the aim of allowing those children with two mums or dads to see their family being accepted.[50]

A similar incident happened a couple of years ago when Muslim parents in Ontario, Canada protested the new sex education curriculum. A curriculum that was approved by some local Toronto Imams![51] Parents were very vocal about their opposition to this curriculum, going as far as to keep their kids away from school until their concerns were addressed. They felt the schools were teaching too much too soon. I think these knee-jerk reactions are motivated by emotion rather than rational thought, and make Muslims appear intolerant. A Muslim Grade 7 student in my past Healthy Relationships afterschool program told me that her mum didn't want me teaching her about the LGBTQ community.

What we must remember is that we are living in inclusive western countries that enshrine the value of 'equality.' In Alberta, legislation has passed that states all schools, even Islamic ones, must provide the space and staff support for a GSA (Gay-Straight Alliance) if requested by a student.

I had never met a gay person in my life until I was an adult. We cannot change Islam to accept homosexuality, but our children are growing up in a different environment. I have seen same-sex couples holding hands in a Junior high, as well as kids transitioning gender. Our children attend school with peers on the LGBTQ spectrum. It is common to hear the words 'girl crush' used to describe a straight girl's crush on another girl. Some Grade 7 Muslim kids I taught stated that if someone is gay, 'so what, it's no big deal.' If you don't discuss this issue, the majority opinion will prevail.

We face discrimination and have an intimate understanding of it; we should not be discriminating against others. We can respect difference, but we don't have to accept it as being permissible. We need to address this issue with our children by being honest. We don't have to understand why people are gay, and the message we give our children can be a simple one.

'A person who is heterosexual or straight is attracted to people of the opposite sex. A person who is gay or homosexual is attracted to people of the same sex. Over the years there has been debate over whether people are born that way or if events that happen in a person's life make them grow up to be gay. Transgender is when someone may be born a boy, but doesn't feel like a boy on the inside. They could be born a girl, but they don't feel like a girl on the inside. It is hard for transgender people to have those feelings. Some transgender people will hide these feelings. Some will start to dress like the other gender and may even have surgery and take medication to change their gender. Gay and transgender people can be bullied and teased for being different. It's important to stand up for them if you ever see this.

Some people love and marry people of the same gender because it is allowed in our country, even though it's not part of our beliefs. As Muslims, we believe that Allah created men and women, so marriage in the eyes of Allah is between a man and a woman. We respect the law of the land that we live in even when it is different to our beliefs and Allah's laws. Islam teaches us to be kind and respectful to people, even when they have different beliefs and lifestyles to ours.' TV shows nowadays are always including a same-sex couple or LGBT character. Even the children's cartoon, My Little Pony, has introduced its first lesbian characters. Luna, a novel about a transgender teen, was selected as a National Book Award Finalist. Marvel Studios (creators of Iron Man, Avengers, Black Panther) plan to bring LGBTQ and transgender characters into their next slate of movies. This topic cannot be avoided. These can be teachable moments which enable you to have open conversations with your child.

I have sat in the sessions of sex education in a junior school. The curriculum is factual, up to date, and has useful resources. Yes, there is no religious framework attached to the information, BUT

- they DO mention that abstinence is the only 100% guaranteed way to avoid STIs and pregnancy.

- they DO say that religious values, family, and cultural beliefs are all reasons that someone may choose abstinence.

- they DO talk about the responsibility of parenthood. Plenty of discussions were had around 'Are you ready for a pregnancy at your age?'

- they DO show pictures of STIs. It is made clear that this can result from having multiple sexual partners.

I do not think parents should pull their children out of these lessons. Before withdrawing your child from sex education classes, ask yourself: 'Do I honestly feel that I have the knowledge, confidence, and commitment to deliver this information to my child?' If the answer is no, then consider yourself a partner with the school. They provide comprehensive information, and you offer the religious values attached to what your children are learning.

The Ontario curriculum has been revised in a positive way for September 2019 and now includes a stronger emphasis on mental health starting from kindergarten. This is important because healthy sexuality is tied to healthy mental health. By Grade 3, children have been introduced to behaviors like vaping and illegal substance use; in Grade 6, masturbation and the harms of pornography are discussed; and in Grade 8, they learn about gender identity (male, female, two-spirit, transgender) and sexual orientation (heterosexual, gay, lesbian, bisexual, pansexual, asexual).[52] We must keep in mind that we are responding to the context we live in.

According to American Muslim organization Heart Women & Girls, even students in Islamic private schools are engaging in sexual activity, including oral sex and homosexual activities. They are doing so without protection or knowledge of the consequences of their behaviour because their schools limit sexual health education to biology and cleanliness. Heart Women & Girls recommends that accurate comprehensive sexual health information be available to all young people through the standardization of sexual health education.[53]

Removing a child from comprehensive sexual health education can be life threatening because of the rise in STIs, as reported by Canadian health agencies. Between 2014 and 2015, HIV diagnoses increased by 17% for 15- to 29-year-olds, which in some cases can turn into a life-or-death situation.[54]

'Parents need to know that all the evidence suggests their children will be much better off, and healthier, being educated about sexual health, relationships, inclusivity, and consent (all of which are included in the Ontario curriculum). Research further suggests that providing sexual health education to young people actually will often result in young people delaying their first sexual experience.'[55]

I'm now going to outline the main material covered by the Alberta sexual health education curriculum and explore how to enhance the information from an Islamic perspective. The full curriculum is available online.[56]

School-aged Children 9-11 (Late elementary)

- Same-sex attachments are still strong at this age.
- They're in the final stages of their gender identity formation.
- Masturbation to orgasm may happen at this stage.
- They're aware of sex differences but have little interest in them.

School Curriculum – Grades 4 - 6

Grade 4 is an introduction to the physical, emotional, and social changes of puberty.

Grade 5 covers fertilization and conception.

Grade 6 students will learn about the risk factors of being sexually active that are associated with blood-borne diseases such as HIV/AIDS, and hepatitis B/C.

How to Support your Child

The pornography conversation needs to start in late elementary school. The harm of pornography is part of the Ontario Grade 6 sexual health curriculum which is sensible. Your child doesn't have to be looking for porn. However, pornography is looking for them, so it is very easy to stumble upon accidentally. You could say, 'There are websites that show adults wearing little or no clothing. It might be an image of a naked person or it could be grown-ups doing adult things. They are not for children's eyes. You need to come and tell me if anything pops up that doesn't feel right or makes you feel uncomfortable so we can talk about it. It is not good for you to look at these things, even though you may want to. You can feel confused because you may feel both yukky and good at the same time. In Islam, decency is important, so that means we lower our gaze (look away) when we see something like this.' There is a very helpful and I believe essential book called *Good Pictures Bad Pictures: Porn-Proofing Today's Young Kids* by Kristen A. Jenson to support this conversation. It is listed in the 'Useful Resources' section at the back of this book.

You don't want to have a conversation for the first time after your child has already seen a graphic display of sexual intercourse or oral sex. It left me heartbroken that my sons were both shown pornography at school. That is why this must be done before they head to junior high. The pornography of today is extreme versions of sex which can traumatize a child. They may not tell you what they've seen because they may feel embarrassed, ashamed, don't want to be asked too many questions, or think you will take away their phone or laptop. It is essential to talk about it before they stumble upon it or are shown it, so they understand what is going on and the risks of watching it. If I had spoken about it to my sons, it would have opened the door for them to come and tell me about that experience.

Even at this young age, there is talk on the playground, and your child is getting some information. If your child doesn't hear any conversation around sexuality at home, they will be incredibly vulnerable to misinformation. Over the decades, the average age where the onset of puberty occurs has gotten younger. Theories suggest different factors such as stress, diet, and increased exposure to endocrine-disrupting chemicals as possible causes. Nine-years-old is a good starting point to explain puberty. Girls may begin to notice the start of puberty, such as soreness or breast buds appearing under the nipples at this age. Keep the explanation simple enough for them to understand it as a positive change that is part of growing up. There are many books around that you may want to use to help start the puberty conversation.

Not all children will ask questions, so make sure to initiate conversations if your child doesn't ask. You may start by commenting on how they've grown, which can lead to, 'As you are growing older, what do you know about the changes that are going to happen to your body?' They may already be receiving (mis)information from outside the home. You can also say, 'You may hear kids talking or joking about sex. Sex is the way Allah has made it possible for us to have children. Sex is a blessing from Allah, but what you hear may not be correct. Do you have any questions right now?' By doing this, you are opening the conversation, if you haven't done it earlier. If they don't want to talk about it, leave it for the moment, but open it up again after a couple of weeks and make sure to have a conversation.

Surround your conversations with your values, those of purity, respect, modesty, honesty, and kindness before the outside influences begin to permeate them. It is equally important to explain why you hold those values and why they should too. 'Because I said so' is not enough; you need to explain the reasons behind the rules. Regular daily prayers should be established by now as a part of family life. If you talk about things from an Islamic perspective, then your children need to see Islam as part of your life, otherwise you lack credibility.

PUBERTY

Puberty can happen for girls any time between 9- and 14-years-old, with the average age being around 11-years-old. Boys can start puberty at about 12-years-old and will have completed puberty by 15- or 16-years-old.

An introduction to puberty could be, 'Allah has made puberty a special time where your body is going to change to become an adult. Everybody develops at their own pace, which may be different from others, and that it is normal. Our body parts will come in different sizes and that's normal. These changes are going to happen over a few years, and some of them can make you feel uncomfortable or embarrassed. These years are difficult because your body is changing but so are your moods. You can quickly go from happy to mad or sad and you may find more drama can happen with friends. The bodies of both girls and boys are getting ready to make it possible for them to become mothers and fathers. Our reproductive organs, also called our sex organs, are going to make this possible. Allah has designed them to work in the most amazing way.

Your body is going to start to release hormones, which are chemicals that cause changes in your body. Not only will physical changes happen, but you will also become more aware of your feelings. Allah makes you begin to notice and like the opposite sex. You may have a crush on someone, where you feel attracted to them. These normal feelings are there so that you can grow up to want to get married and have those feelings for your husband or wife. You may see your peers develop romantic relationships which don't usually last long.'

This is the time to talk about lowering your gaze, modesty and awrah. Don't react negatively if your child mentions a crush on someone, because you want to keep the channels of communication open. Remind them though to limit contact with their 'crush.'

Also, let your children know that once puberty begins, they now become accountable for their deeds. Giving them a nice new prayer mat, tasbih and a book on Islam or their own Qur'an will give them a feeling of maturity and responsibility.

Acknowledge Changes and Feelings

Discuss the physical, social, and emotional changes of puberty for both boys and girls.

Physical changes girls need to be made aware of include:

- growing taller, reaching adult height around 16 years
- breast development – be aware that she may feel self-conscious about needing to start wearing a bra
- pubic and underarm hair
- sweating more, body odor
- hips widening
- increased hunger and weight gain
- vaginal discharge
- oilier skin
- menstruation
- the need for more sleep

For boys, make them aware of:

- increased growth (growth spurt around 13-years of age)
- broadening shoulders
- muscles develop
- pubic/underarm hair
- body and facial hair
- voice cracking and deepening
- private parts grow bigger
- the production of sperm
- they may have erections and ejaculate

Keep close tabs on your children so that you can check-in for any questions they may have and keep tabs on how they are feeling.

A conversation about regular hair removal and the increased need for hygiene in the form of daily showers and deodorant is necessary at this time. More active sebaceous glands can cause pimples and acne, so a good skincare routine is needed. If your daughter is curious about her private parts, give her a mirror to take a look. It is important for girls to know and understand their body.

As parents, it's important for us to remember that besides the physical changes of puberty, there are also emotional changes. Acne and mood changes are happening at the same time as peers becoming more judgmental. Be understanding, patient, and give them some space. They are not trying to be difficult but rather are having difficulty trying to cope.

You can use a book about puberty or get some cartoon-like drawings to explain their reproductive systems. Boys and girls should also learn about each other's bodies. Use this teaching experience to marvel at how wondrous Allah has made our body. Girls need to be made aware of their vulva, vagina, clitoris, cervix, uterus, fallopian tubes, and ovaries, as well as the functions of all these body parts. Boys need to be made aware of their scrotum, testicles, penis, and their internal organs as well, such as the epididymis, seminal vesicle and vas deferens. The Alberta curriculum uses the site www.teachingsexualhealth.ca for their lessons and is an excellent overall comprehensive site that includes diagrams that can facilitate this topic. There are also Christian-based books, such as God's Design for Sex series, which cover puberty while maintaining a spiritual element for all explanations.

MENSTRUATION

Menstruation is a topic that must be discussed with your daughters early enough that when they begin menstruating, they are not scared or worried and understand what is happening. You could explain menstruation like this: 'It is Allah's way of getting a woman's body ready to be able to carry a baby one day. It is a sign that you can get pregnant. Every month your ovaries will release an egg. This is called ovulation. Just before it's released, the uterus builds up a thicker lining of blood and tissue. If the egg is fertilized, it will need this lining to have a place to grow into a baby. If the egg is not fertilized, that thicker lining will break down and dribble out the body through the vagina. The same thing will happen every month. A menstrual period lasts anywhere from 3 to 7 days on average. Some girls call menstruation a 'period' or 'time of the month.' When girls first start menstruating, it can be irregular for up to a year or longer before it is regular.' The fiqh of menstruation is not covered in this book but there are courses, books and online resources that cover it in detail.

Talk about cramps, sanitary pads, and tampons and explain that a ghusl is where the whole body is washed in a certain way after the menstrual bleeding has finished so they can be ready to start praying again. Explain to your daughter(s) that some girls or women will experience some discomfort such as tender breasts, fluid retention and cramps which can be mild to painful. The use of muscle relaxants, painkillers, hot water bottles, or a heating pad can help, as can gentle exercise. There are also natural remedy alternatives. Explain that tampons are tightly woven absorbent material shaped like a tube and inserted into the vagina to soak up the menstrual blood. The issue I have with tampons is the fact that they are keeping blood inside the body and contain chemicals (unless you use organic ones). Make sure your daughter is aware that tampons must be changed at least every 4 hours during the day or there is a risk of toxic shock syndrome. Have her keep spare clothing and some pads in her locker at school. Explain that she is exempt from prayers and fasting while on her period. Fasts have to be made up but not prayers.

I would make boys aware of periods before they go to junior high or middle school, at around 12-years-old. Boys need to learn to respect the changes of a woman's body, and menstruation should not be hidden as something shameful or dirty. I have heard of girls having to go through suhoor and pretend they are fasting to avoid the shame. Sometimes girls have bad cramps or heavy periods where they may become low on iron. They shouldn't have to compromise on meeting their nutritional needs when they are exempt from fasting.

Boys need to be taught the modesty of not asking a female why she isn't fasting or praying because menstruation has been normalized in the home. Remember, your boys one day will be men, and we want them to not be shy around their daughters when it comes to a regular monthly function. We also want our sons to have empathy for the difficulties that menstruation brings, whether these are cramps or mood changes. Possessing this knowledge encourages respect for the way that Allah has made us.

We have the example of the Prophet (PBUH) who did not shame Aisha during her menstrual period. He remained affectionate towards her during this time by laying with her and caressing her.

ERECTIONS

Boys have the ability to get an erection from early childhood, as I discovered with having two sons. Erections will become more frequent once they reach puberty, and they can happen anywhere and at any time, which is also normal. You can explain that 'you will start to have more erections at this time, which happens to all boys and is normal. It can happen when you touch your penis or watch something on TV that makes you feel happy, or while you are dreaming, or you see someone attractive. Sometimes it just happens for no reason. It often happens when you wake up in the morning. This is when your penis gets bigger and can become hard, because more blood is going there. You are also starting to make sperm now. Your testicles produce sperm which travels down the epididymis and is stored in the vas deferens. These erections are Allah's way of getting your body ready for changing into becoming a man.'

NOCTURNAL EMISSION (WET DREAMS)

Explain wet dreams before your son is likely start having them. Wet dreams are not necessarily related to erotic fantasies or masturbation (though they can be). Wet dreams vary in how often they occur.

A conversation about the changes of puberty may already have happened or can happen at the same time that you begin a conversation about wet dreams. Should you be discussing both, you can then include, 'When you go through puberty, your body will make a hormone (a chemical that causes changes) called testosterone, which is going to make you have erections more often. An erection can happen at anytime. You are also making sperm now that mixes with fluid and is then called semen. Allah is getting your body used to making sperm and your semen will build up. When it needs to be released, you will have an ejaculation while you're asleep. This is when the semen comes out of your penis, which happens to many boys and is normal. It amounts to about a teaspoon that comes out. If you see or feel wetness on your pajamas or sheets, then you need to have a ghusl. This is called a wet dream, because it happens while you are asleep.'

Teach your son about ghusl and keep a spare set of sheets in his room so he can change his bed himself and avoid embarrassment.

Though not as common, it is also possible for girls to have wet dreams. If there is discharge, similar to that which occurs with an orgasm, then your daughter would also need to have a ghusl.

CONCEPTION AND FERTILIZATION

Intercourse is covered in Grade 5/aged 10-years-old. You need to explain it before your child heads to junior high/middle school because you don't want them to get the crude or porn version first. Acknowledge that what you are describing may sound gross, and explain that when they are older, their feelings about this act will change because they will understand that it's a good thing from Allah. Allah puts love between a husband and wife and encourages us to have children.

'A husband and wife will lie close together and hug each other so their bodies can come together. Allah designed their private parts to fit together like a lock and key. Allah makes our private parts very sensitive, so it feels nice for them when this happens and makes them love each other more. All the cuddling and closeness makes a man's penis become firmer and a woman's vagina become moist. This makes it easy for the husband's penis to go into his wife's vagina. This is called sexual intercourse. The excitement builds causing the husband to ejaculate, which means the semen leaves his body and goes into his wife's body and swims up into the fallopian tube to find an egg. When the sperm joins itself to an egg, it's called fertilization. The fertilized egg, which is called a zygote, will travel down into the uterus and settles into the womb so it can grow into a baby. It goes from being called a zygote to an embryo and then becomes a fetus. The wife's belly gets bigger because the baby is growing every day. Food comes to the baby from a cord that attaches from the baby's belly button to its Mummy. The baby starts as a very tiny seed but grows for nine months, and then when he/she is ready to be born, the Mummy pushes them out. Babies can be born at home or in a hospital. It is a miracle from Allah that this is how life starts.'

This can also be the age to explain how childbirth has given mothers a special place in Islam. 'Having a baby is hard work. Allah has made a mother special to be able to carry a baby inside her body for nine months. By the 9th month, it gets hard to walk and sleep, and she is very tired.

When she is ready to give birth, she has to work extra hard to push her baby out.' The Qur'an also mentions the fact that 'In pain did his mother bear him, and in pain did she give him birth' (46:15).

Abu Hurairah (May Allah be pleased with him) reported: 'A person came to Messenger of Allah (PBUH) and asked, "Who among people is most deserving of my fine treatment?" He (PBUH) said, "Your mother." He again asked, "Who next?" "Your mother," the Prophet (PBUH) replied again. He asked, "Who next?" He (the Prophet (PBUH)) said again, "Your mother." He again asked, "Then who?" Thereupon he (PBUH) said, "Then your father"' (Al-Bukhari and Muslim, Book 1, Hadith 316).

Tips for Strengthening the Parent-Child Bond

Continue with the concept of connection before correction and keep the channels of communication open. It becomes much easier to have more in-depth talks when you regularly plug into daily conversations. As your children begin to experience puberty, having a strong connection will make it easier to ask them about the challenges they are facing and ask them how you can help.

Individual time and family meetings are both really important to keep on top of issues and remain connected to your child.

Adolescence, 12-14 years

They will start to withdraw from you and can feel confused, self-conscious and embarrassed about puberty.
- Same sex attachments are still of primary importance.
- They may masturbate, sometimes to orgasm.
- They can also begin accessing pornography by choice.

These years are no doubt the start of the most challenging period, because teens are trying to formulate an identity, peers take on a more prominent role in their lives, and your kids are then distancing themselves from you.

School Curriculum – Grades 7-9

Grade 7 – Puberty is addressed, as well as the effects of media and culture on sexuality and gender roles. The curriculum examines abstinence and the decision to postpone sexual activity as a healthy choice.

Grade 8 – Abuse (physical, emotional, and sexual abuse), common STIs (chlamydia, HPV, herpes, gonorrhea, hepatitis B/C, and HIV) and basic contraception (abstinence, condoms, foam, and birth control pills) are all taught. The responsibilities and consequences associated with involvement in a sexual relationship are also addressed.

Grade 9 – Safer sex practices (including abstinence), the consequences of sexual assault on victims, pregnancy and parenting responsibilities, and how to reduce sexual risk (e.g. assertive behaviour) are all discussed.

How to Support your Child

Puberty involves many emotional changes, and you should keep the communication open and continuous to support this. Be an askable adult and remind them that they can come to you with questions and you'll be there when they need you. Your teen will still have many questions that they may think about, but not ask.

Continue the conversations about puberty, masturbation (covered in a later section), wet dreams, and menstruation as needed with this age group. Peer pressure becomes more intense at this age, and cyberbullying is also a concern. The need to fit in becomes stronger. Normalize their feelings by telling them your own stories of times when you felt pressured, angry, sad, overwhelmed, and tempted. Teens require a great deal of affection and praise as they're going through this phase, but also require reasonable and fair limits.

Youths should be made aware of the consequences of sexting and sending nudes, which starts to happen at this age. This has also led to the desensitization of kids to sexualized images. It needs to be made clear that forwarding a nude photo that someone sends you is illegal, and the correct action is to delete these photos immediately. Explain the importance of not succumbing to pressure to send a nude because you lose control of what happens to that photo once you press send. Sexting is online flirting but can be the start of making bad choices.

Dating can start at this age, and you can adapt the conversation about why dating isn't allowed from the information in the section for 15-to 17-year-olds. If they talk about having a crush on someone, do make them aware that they need to take care with this information. In the age of social media, their feelings can soon become widespread knowledge and affect a reputation.

They should also be made aware of contraception and STIs (sexually transmitted infections).

CONTRACEPTION

An explanation of this concept to your children may take this form: 'In Islam, sex is a blessing and a way that a husband and wife show love and grow love. Sex is not just for making a baby, so contraception is allowed. This stops a pregnancy from happening if a couple doesn't feel they are ready to start their family yet. There are many types, and some of the names you will hear are: the birth control pill, the ring, the implant, a condom, spermicides, a diaphragm, an IUD, an injection, a patch, a cervical cap, a sponge and the withdrawal method. None of these methods are 100% effective, but most are 99% effective. A couple will talk and decide together what method of contraception they think is best for them to use.'

STIs – SEXUALLY TRANSMITTED INFECTIONS

The conversation around STIs could be along the lines of: 'Allah wants us to be married before we have sex, which keeps us safe. When people have sex outside of marriage, they may have more than one partner, which increases the risk of getting a STI. Sometimes people don't even know they have a STI and can unknowingly pass it on. If the STI doesn't get treated early, it could make it difficult for you to have children later.

'The most common STI among teens is called chlamydia, which you can also get from oral sex. There are others, such as syphilis and gonorrhea, which can have serious side effects, including blindness, if untreated. You will hear about having "safe sex," where the boy will use a condom to stop the spread of any STIs. This is safer but it is still not safe sex. Sex outside marriage is never safe. A condom can break, and you could still end up with a STI or get pregnant. Allah doesn't want you to be scared of a STI or of pregnancy when you have sex, which is why He says to wait until you are married. Contraception may be almost 99% effective, but you could be in the 1% where it fails, and you become pregnant.'

Tips to Strengthen the Parent-Child Bond

Family meetings - In addition to spending time together as a family, have weekly 20-minute family meetings to share your values and expectations, and to solve any problems. Avoid lecturing and keep these sessions positive through appreciating each other, in order to build self-esteem. Teens need to feel valued and loved. Give them some monthly individual time to do a shared, enjoyable activity. Individual time should also be between mothers and sons and dads and daughters. There has been much written about the importance of a father-daughter relationship in promoting self-esteem.

Friends - Our children must socialize with friends that share common values. Get to know their friends by welcoming them into your home. Make your home the one where kids want to hang out. There isn't always much we can do if we don't like our children's friends. Forcing your children to stop associating with certain friends that you don't like will only cause them to rebel. We can point out concerns and try to widen their circle of friends through school and sports activities, youth halaqas, and youth groups. Make them aware of the hadith: 'Therefore let every one of you carefully consider the company he keeps' (at-Tirmidhi 2378). I reminded my sons that in a friendship, each person influences the other. Think about whether your friends are a positive influence or not.

Stay connected to your community - Encourage activities where your children can build a group of Muslim friends to create a supportive network for them. Pray together regularly and teach them about du'a. Remind them that Allah is always watching and knows what they are doing and saying. Be balanced in presenting Allah as a kind and merciful God while also reminding them of Allah's punishment. Being too hard on children can cause them to feel resentment towards Allah.

Late Teens - 15-17 years

- This is both an exciting and stressful time for late teens who are starting to define their own personal values.
- Their emotions are still quickly changeable.
- There is an increased desire for intimacy, and they may masturbate.

During adolescence, we should explain that 'sometimes we can feel an attraction for the same sex. It doesn't necessarily mean you are gay, but it can feel confusing. Attraction to the same sex is not sinful, but as Muslims, we are not supposed to act on those feelings.'

I found these years as a parent difficult because you feel like you are losing control. Your teens are becoming more independent. They are now going to movies on their own, getting together with friends more, and their peers start dating and getting involved in relationships. My sons had no Muslim friends until their late teens. We lived in a small Muslim community, and there were no boys their age in our social circles. They were now being invited to parties, and I wasn't always 100% sure how much parental supervision there would be. My thinking was that they had to learn how to navigate these tricky situations while I could have some input into it, rather than forbid them from going, which would cause resentment. I knew they would have the freedom to do these things when they left for university, so I did allow them to go to parties. It provided opportunities for many good conversations about alcohol, drugs, and relationships. Before they went out, I reminded them that '… Allah is aware of what you do' (Qur'an 24:30).

Then came the desire to go clubbing once they turned 18. Again, I knew I couldn't control their social lives once they went to university, so I did allow them to go. I did say that I wasn't happy about it and we are accountable for how we spend our time, but I also feel that if something becomes forbidden fruit, it becomes more desirable. Again, it paved the way for conversations about explicit music, alcohol, hooking up, and so on. I felt that I had more opportunity to discuss why these things are not good for our soul because they had seen them firsthand. I could have told them they couldn't go, but they could still have gone and lied to me about their whereabouts. I wanted to encourage honesty and know where they were. Our children are sometimes going to do things which we would prefer they didn't do. For myself, I let those things go and remembered the bigger picture: helping them not cross the red line. Alhamdullilah, they outgrew the interest in going to clubs.

I would have preferred that they had Muslim friends and had a youth group at the Masjid to fill in the gap for socializing, but that wasn't their reality. They did not have Muslim friends, and normal behavior for their friends was drugs, drinking, and dating. From the time my sons were young, I regularly talked about accountability to Allah so even though they did go to parties and clubs, they held on to their core values of faith. I responded to the context of their lives but by no means am I suggesting that partying or clubbing is okay from an Islamic perspective. My non-Muslim best friend whose sons were the same ages and friends with my boys reassured me that my sons didn't drink. That information came from her sons. I say this so that you know that what you do in your home is of the utmost importance.

School Curriculum – Grades 10-12

This age group will be examining commitment and intimacy, and values and trust in relationships. They will also look at healthy sexuality, responsible sexual behaviour and respectful sexual expression. They will explore how personal values influence choices and assess the consequences of being sexually active, all of which is necessary information.

How to Support your Child

Have conversations about the following topics. I have placed these topics in the late teens section because of the level of detail included. Take note that a simpler version of these conversations should be had with middle schoolers.

MASTURBATION

Many boys and girls do masturbate, though it is more common in boys. You will likely have seen your young child discovering that fondling their genitals or rubbing against furniture creates a sensation that they like. They are pre-pubertal, so I wouldn't get into an Islamic conversation about it or shame your child. I would say, 'We don't touch our private parts in public' and use distraction with alternative activities. If they do play with themselves in public, a gentle 'We don't do that here' is enough.

You should talk about masturbation around the time puberty is arriving (around 10- to 12-years-old for boys), unless your child asks you something about it before that age. I would explain it by saying that 'sometimes people will use their hands to rub their private parts because they like the way it feels. This is called self-pleasuring or masturbation.'

The Qur'an does not explicitly mention masturbation. However, there is a verse, which some scholars say is referring to masturbation and other scholars say is referring to adultery. The verse in question mentions '…those whose desires exceed those limits are transgressors' (23: 5-7).

The majority opinion considers masturbation a disliked act which may be permitted in exceptional circumstances where someone feels he will commit Zina; or is finding it difficult to get married and is sexually frustrated and needs to release sexual tension. Masturbation can also be used to cope with stress, so keep yourself plugged into your kids' moods so that you can see if they are struggling. Their level of maturity can decide how deep you go into the information.

Let them know that 'Allah made our private parts with many nerve endings, which makes them very sensitive. When touched, it can give you good feelings which we call feeling aroused. Masturbation is something you do to yourself, but sex is something special that Allah made for a man and a woman to experience together. We are meant to share our bodies with our husband or wife, and find pleasure together, not on our own.

'Masturbation can lead to an orgasm, which is an intense feeling of pleasure that happens, and you will ejaculate at that time. An orgasm is also called a climax, because it's the best feeling that you get from sex. Allah has made an orgasm, also called "coming" to be the ultimate experience when a husband and wife have intercourse. That's how it should happen instead of you doing it to yourself.

'Sexual attraction is healthy and something Allah made a part of us. It is also powerful. Masturbation can quickly become a habit. You can start to fantasize, where you escape in your mind and have sexual thoughts about a girl. You can start to spend too much time thinking about it or doing it, and then some people take it a step further and want to look at images of naked people while doing it.

This is unhealthy and not good for your mental health and can affect a future relationship. If you need help to stop, don't feel embarrassed to say so. It will feel like a challenge but playing a sport, board games, socializing, praying, and making du'a will all help with this. We fast to develop self-control, and we must try to resist temptation with this too. This is where lowering our gaze is essential. Don't look at images of attractive girls online. If you are feeling lonely or frustrated, get up and pray. Islam encourages us to get married young because it is normal to have these urges and interests and when you are married, you can satisfy them.'

With young adult children, you can encourage voluntary fasting. It will bring them closer to Allah and it also reduces the sex drive. The Prophet, (PBUH) said, 'Those who cannot (marry) should fast, for it is a means of cooling sexual passion' (Sahih Muslim, Book 8, Hadith 3231).

ORAL SEX/ANAL SEX

The most commonly asked question by Muslim youth in Grades 7-12 pertains to oral sex. Questions range from 'What is it?' to (more commonly) 'Is it haram?'

Unfortunately, we are living in a time where we are having conversations of an explicit nature with younger children than in previous eras, because we don't want peers or porn giving our children a vulgar version of the truth. There are also Muslim teens participating in oral sex, thinking it still preserves their virginity because it is not intercourse.

My response to these questions was 'Oral sex is where a person uses their mouth to stimulate their partner's genitals, which may sound strange or even gross. Remember that Allah helps love to grow between the hearts of a husband and wife, and they will bring their bodies together in different ways to show love and feel good. This is one way of doing that. Sex is an expression of love and commitment. Every part of our body is a blessing and a gift from our Creator.'

For high schoolers, I elaborated and let them know that 'there are different opinions on oral sex, but the majority opinion is that it is permissible in marriage based on the verse "Your wives are as a tilth unto you so approach your tilth when or how ye will"(Qur'an 2:223).

'In Islam, all sexual practices are permitted except those expressly prohibited, which are anal sex or sex while a woman is menstruating. All sexual relations must be by mutual agreement (taradi) and consensual. While spouses must fulfill the reasonable sexual needs of their spouse, they do not have to engage in any activity that makes them feel uncomfortable.'

PORNOGRAPHY

The unfortunate reality is that it's not a question of if but rather when your child will stumble across pornography. Pornhub, the most popular and largest hardcore porn website today received 33.5 billion site visits in 2018.[57] Imagine that number is only one website and there are hundreds of thousands of other sites.

According to 90% of teens and 96% of young adults, conversations with friends about porn are encouraged, accepted, or neutral. Not recycling is considered more immoral than porn.[58]

In 2007, a University of Alberta study of 13 and 14-year-old students (429 in total) from 17 schools across Alberta found that 90% of boys and 70% of girls had seen explicit content at least once and 1 in 3 boys were heavy porn users.[59] In 2019, a clinical psychologist and certified sex therapist found that 'many teens and young people are consuming an increasing amount of pornography in Alberta.'[60] It is disheartening to imagine what that statistic may look like now and these are the peers of your children or may even be your child. Worryingly, only 38% of 16- to 17-year-olds said their parents taught them about pornography according to research by the Sex Education Forum.[61]

Before your child reaches middle school/junior high, you need to have had a conversation about pornography. Our children must be taught the skills necessary to avoid pornography because they are not equipped to deal with the pull of it. The book *Good Pictures Bad Pictures* is excellent for teaching this skill (see useful resources section). Porn can rewire a brain. Imagine the impact of pornography on a child's developing brain which lacks judgement and impulse control.

Kids are going to be accessing the internet, and even with parental controls in place, it is still possible to view porn on a home computer, laptop, smartphone or through someone else. Remember that your child's Xbox, PlayStation, Wii, iPad, also gives them internet access. Porn bots have infiltrated gaming systems like Xbox and PlayStation and these bots are there to lure your kids into viewing porn, so safety features must be set up on them.[62] The largest pornography company in the world has invested in becoming a video game platform distributing some free-to-view pornographic games. Since no credit card is needed, your child can easily access these games. Animated porn is no less harmful than the real thing.[63]

What are you doing to monitor your kid's smartphones when they aren't home? At the school I work at, a large number of junior high kids spend their lunch hours glued to their phones. You can't control everything but you can talk about porn so your children are prepared for what they will see and fight the pull of it.

Check out the 'Useful Resources' section at the back of the book for information on good digital parenting.

For junior high/middle school kids, you can provide an explanation similar to this: 'Pornography comes in different forms. It can be cartoons, images or videos where people are wearing little to no clothing. Sometimes their private parts may be shown, and they will behave in a sexual way. However, this sexual behaviour is not in a healthy or kind way that Allah meant it to be. Some people like to look at things like that because it makes them feel good. They get tingly feelings, which is called getting aroused. When you see pornography, it can make you feel like you shouldn't look because it feels wrong, and at the same time, you may find it hard to stop watching. It makes your brain want to keep looking and it can be so powerful, you can't stop. It is natural to be curious and porn is taking advantage of that. Pornography actually hurts your brain because it will make certain parts of your brain overwork. This changes your brain and can cause you to become depressed. Shaytaan will whisper, "You can stop anytime," but this is not true. It can become something you want to look at everyday which is called an addiction. Allah tells us in the Qur'an surah 4, verse 28 that "...man was created weak." It takes strength to battle against our nafs (desires). We control it or it will control us. Shaytaan connects to us through our nafs. You might see something pop up while you are on the computer. If this happens, look away and tell yourself, "this is porn and it's a slippery slope to messing me up." Then please come and tell me so we can talk about it. What you saw may stick in your mind, so you have to make a du'a and ask Allah to help you think of something else. Read A'oodhu Billahi min al-Shaitan ir-rajeem. You want protection "From the mischief of the Whisperer (Of Evil)..." Shaytaan (Qur'an 114:5).

'Watching pornography is harmful to our mental and emotional health. What you will see is not how a relationship or sex is meant to be. These two people don't love each other and might be complete strangers to one another. They might even hurt each other and act like that's normal.

Usually it's women who are hurt. Sometimes women and girls are sold into pornography and forced to do this, which is sad. We are helping more women and girls get sold into pornography if we keep watching. When you keep watching this over and over, you can become addicted to it. You will then find it very hard to have a healthy relationship one day because you won't know how to be with a real person anymore. Allah wants you to have a happy and healthy relationship, which includes healthy sex. Porn will ruin it. Sex is a private and loving thing that Allah wants a married couple to enjoy. It is not meant to be watched. It is not allowed in Islam, and we have to remember that Allah watches everything that we do.'

It is vital that your children also see you lower your gaze when indecent images or inappropriate scenes are portrayed on TV. You should be modeling this. You can also bring up why these kinds of scenes are inappropriate.

We can't think 'our children' wouldn't do things like this because that simply isn't true. Good kids also get pulled into porn. Their biological nature is responding to a stimulus that is powerful and enticing. Muslim kids are not only watching porn but are even experiencing porn addiction. I've come across 14-year-old polite masjid-attending Muslim boys watching porn in the classroom. When my younger son was moving away to go to university, I strongly encouraged him to sign up to be paired with Muslim roommates thinking he was safer from outside influences. I was wrong. One of them watched porn on a daily basis.

My older son's university roommates were the same. My son had put a filter on the TV but was pressured to remove it for porn consumption. My sons were part of their university MSAs and took part in Jummah, iftaars and various events. I asked them if they knew any Muslim boys who didn't watch porn. Sadly, the response was 'No, they all watch porn.' The most important factors cited in reducing porn use in children is a warm and communicative parent-child relationship. Other constructive influences are sex education and open parent-child communication about sexual and media experiences.[64]

We leave our Muslim children very vulnerable and more likely to watch porn if we don't talk about it. Adolescents are naturally curious and if you haven't satisfied that curiosity, you leave them open to porn addiction. Knowing what's right doesn't stop one from doing wrong. Even those with strong faith experience temptation. We have to remember that Shaytaan has made his intentions clear in the Qur'an surah 7 verses 16-17. 'I will lie in wait for them on Thy Straight Way: Then will I assault them from before them and behind them, from their right and their left.'

Search the internet and you will find neurological research that suggests that viewing pornography can shrink areas of the brain as well as deplete certain chemicals which are overused through activating the pleasure centre. It also increases feelings of loneliness and depression. It distorts sex into something for recreation which the viewer normalizes making them more likely to accept and participate in premarital sex.

The worst part of addiction is the fact that the user develops a tolerance over time and therefore must start viewing more hardcore porn to feel the same high. This depraved view of sex is detrimental to one's well-being and a future healthy relationship and marriage.

So, what should you do if you find out your child is watching pornography?

Stay calm, despite feeling betrayed and disappointed. Put yourself in the right frame of mind before you start the conversation. You can't be emotional and go in crying to your child with comments like 'How could you do this?' 'What were you thinking?' or 'We can't trust you.' Take some time to collect your thoughts, pray two rakaats of nafl salaah, make du'a, and then go in. Keep communication open so you can help them if it's already become an addiction or help them stop it from becoming one. This will only happen if you don't shame them. If you do condemn them, they won't speak to you about it which leaves you not knowing if they have gone back to it.

You can start with, 'Based on the computer history, it appears that you have been searching sites with explicit adult content. We need to talk about the risks to you of watching this material.'

Resist the temptation to lecture and instead ask questions and listen. Ask them how and when it started, how often they view it and how they feel when they watch it. It may take more than one conversation to get all the facts. If they were masturbating while watching, there is more brain neuronal involvement which would strengthen the addiction. Your child may be relieved that they do not have to carry this alone. Help them understand that they have your support. Any addiction is difficult to overcome, and it will be a struggle to stop watching it. Remind them of the Hadith Qudsi where Allah says, 'If he comes to Me walking, I go to him running' (Bukhari 7536). Allah wants us to turn to him and repent so 'Do not despair of the mercy of Allah. Indeed Allah forgives all sins' (Qur'an 39:53).

Remind them that you love them and want to help them. Explain that you understand that their curiosity got them in over their heads. Remind them that sex is a blessing that's private, and of Allah's mercy when repenting. Support them by keeping them from being isolated or tempted. Continue checking in and use accountability software for porn. Help is also available from 'Purify Your Gaze,' the online program for Muslims suffering porn addiction, or a counselor.

When I delivered presentations to high schoolers on sex, dating, and relationships, the sessions were well attended, with most students stating that this topic was not discussed at home. In engaging with teens, take care not to lecture or overuse the word 'haram' because your teen will stop listening.

Below is an outline of the sessions I presented to high schoolers. The introduction started with the idea that to love and be loved in return is a basic, universal human need. This is in the Qur'an: '... And He has put love and mercy between your (hearts)...' (30:21).

WHAT IS THE ISLAMIC VIEW ON SEXUALITY?

- In Islam, there is no unnatural celibacy. We have been made with sexual desire.

- Sex is an expression of love, and in Islam, its purpose is not just for procreation; therefore, birth control (contraception) is permissible. Sexual desire is something special that Allah has put in our hearts and bodies, for which we are thankful.

- Sex has health benefits: improved immunity, heart health, pain relief, stress reduction, and the release of love hormones to bond with a spouse.

- Sex is not just a physical act but also an emotional and spiritual one. It is an important part of a marriage that must be nurtured. Sex is an extraordinary gift from Allah and is meant to be enjoyable. It is not 'dirty' but must be treated with respect and is something to be protected.

- Sex is considered an act of charity in Islam, and so you earn blessings when you have sex with your spouse.

- It is sunnah to make a du'a before starting intercourse, which shows us how sacred this act of intimacy is. 'In the name of Allah. O Allah, keep Shaytaan away from us, and keep Shaytaan away from (the offspring) which You grant us' (Bukhari 141 & Muslim 1434).

- Prophet Muhammad (PBUH) did not shy away from talking about sexual matters. He even talked about the importance of foreplay, and he was playful with his wives.

- The Prophet (PBUH) obliged spouses to fulfill the sexual desires of one another. In Islam, sexual pleasure is for both men and women.

This desire is meant to be satisfied within a marital relationship. The first relationship on earth was between a husband and a wife. We are not created to be alone. Marriage is fulfilling half our religion and is the foundation of family life, as mentioned in Surah 2 verse 35 in the Qur'an 'O Adam! Dwell thou and thy wife in the Garden...'

A common question from high schoolers was, 'Does sex hurt?' I replied, 'It can be uncomfortable the first time because you may feel nervous or anxious, which is why our Prophet (PBUH) discouraged intercourse without foreplay. Foreplay is the romance, caressing and kissing to get you in the mood, or sexually aroused, which is often lacking in what you see on TV or movies. Foreplay is important to the whole experience of sex and is recommended in Islam. Allah designed a woman's body to produce a lubricant when she is aroused, to ensure that it isn't painful. You are supposed to enjoy sex by taking the time for foreplay. A husband and wife are both supposed to please each other, which brings them closer and keeps them in love.'

PREMARITAL SEX IN THE QUR'AN AND HADITH

Premarital sex is considered a major sin in Islam (as well as in Christianity and Judaism). There are Qur'anic verses that make this clear, and these were shared with the students. I was asked beforehand to provide Qur'anic verses.

Qur'an

- The surah called The Believers mentions they are those 'who abstain from sex except to those joined to them in the marriage bond...' (23:5-6).

- 'And those who guard their chastity, except with their wives...' (70:29/30).

- 'Such will be the honoured ones in the Gardens (of Bliss)' (70:35).

- Believing men and women should 'lower their gaze and guard their modesty...' (24:30-31).

- 'Those who invoke not with God any other god, nor slay such life as God Has made sacred, except for just cause, nor commit Fornication; - any that does This (not only) meets punishment (But) the Penalty on the Day of Judgment will be doubled to him, and he will dwell Therein in ignominy' (25:68-69).

- 'For men and women who guard their chastity and for men and women who engage much in God's praise, for them has God prepared forgiveness and great reward' (33:35).

Hadith

- The Prophet (PBUH) also reportedly said, 'Whenever a man is alone with a woman, Shaytan is the third among them' (at-Tirmidhi, Vol. 4, Book 7, Hadith 2165). When young people are getting to know each other, being alone together is a great temptation toward wrongdoing.

POSITIVE MESSAGE

Teens must get the positive message that premarital sex is a sin because Allah is trying to protect them. I stressed the point that 'A great reward is promised to you if you guard your chastity. We cannot imagine what that great reward even looks like, as we do not know the full miracle of what Allah is capable of. Allah knows that it is hard; that's why you will be rewarded in this manner.'

ALLAH'S PROTECTION

'So how is Allah trying to protect you from the consequences of premarital sex?
There are four aspects to your health – physical, mental/emotional, social, and spiritual. A sexual relationship affects all four of these aspects.' Here are some points you can direct to your children regarding their health.

Physical Sexually Transmitted Infections (STIs)

Teens are the group at the highest risk of STIs. The most common STI is chlamydia, but recently, there was an outbreak of syphilis in Alberta which saw a tenfold increase since 2014. If a person misses out on early treatment because they don't know they have a STI, they are at risk of complications. There are many different STIs out there. There is a saying that when you have sex with someone, you are having sex with all the partners they've had. The more partners they've had, the higher the chances of them having a STI and possibly passing it on to you. There is no safe sex, only safer sex. No contraception is 100% effective. You can only lower your chances of pregnancy or STI, not remove the possibility entirely.

Pregnancy

For a married couple in a committed relationship, having a baby is a different experience than a teen pregnancy. For a teen,

- your education may be put on hold.

- the chances of raising a child on a low income are high.

- you will have a higher risk of depression than a more mature mother.

- your friends will be carrying on with school or college/university while you are isolated and raising a child. Your friends will be in a different stage of life to you and will start to lose interest in your company because you no longer share common interests.

- you may be a single parent, because not all teen dads stick around. Are you ready for that?

- you may end up putting your baby up for adoption or even abandoning them because you don't feel you can look after them. Your baby won't have gotten the kind of start in life that Allah would have wanted them to have. That's why Allah wants you to wait to commit yourself to one special person that you marry before you have a baby, so he/she has the best start in life.

- having to get married because you are pregnant is not the best start to a marriage.

- intercourse before age 18 increases the risk of cervical cancer, as does having multiple partners.

- pregnancy at this young age has a higher rate of having a premature or low birth-weight baby.

- pregnancy has a higher risk of physical and emotional problems for the mother.

- your brain only fully develops between 21- and 25-years-old. Are you ready to be a parent?'

Discuss the responsibilities of being a parent with your child. Do they babysit? Have they looked after a baby for any length of time? Have them imagine that 24/7 at their age.

Mental/Emotional

- Sex is not just a physical experience but also an emotional one. If you break up, you may experience feelings of loneliness, stress, loss, depression, and rejection. You may feel guilt and regret upon realizing that you shared your body in the most intimate of all experiences with someone with whom you are now disconnected. If you break up, do you think the chances are high that you will say, 'I'm happy we had sex'? On the flip side, some people may not regret that choice, but they tend to be the exception to the rule.

- An unexpected pregnancy can lead to an abortion and ending a life can lead to feelings of guilt which can last a lifetime.

- Once you start on the road to having sex with a boyfriend or girlfriend and then break up, it becomes much easier to do the same when you start a new relationship. This can impact your mental/emotional health because you are allowing your body to be used by more than one partner, which can lower your self-esteem.

Social

- You may have exchanged explicit/nude photos or videos within your relationship, which can be shared after a breakup which would damage your reputation. Unfortunately, the double standard still exists, which is wrong and unfair, but girls are still judged differently than boys. Girls are often described as 'slut' 'easy' or 'she puts out'. A girl may find herself shunned by other girls, and boys may objectify and talk negatively about her.

Spiritual

- Dating will take you away from obeying and remembering Allah. As your attraction to a person grows, your thoughts, emotions, and time are going to be focused on this love interest. The same thing happens when you marry, but then you have committed to a life that includes Allah, so it does not impact your spirituality in the same way.

DISPELLING MYTHS

Teens still believe some myths about pregnancy, so these have to be dispelled. The truth is:

- You can get pregnant the first time you have sex, regardless of position.

- Standing upright after sex does not stop a pregnancy.

- Even without intercourse, you can get pregnant if your partner ejaculates near your vagina. It is not common, but it can happen.

It is important for you as a parent to reflect on whether you are holding on to any outdated cultural myths and traditions. Some prevalent myths worth mentioning are:

- a girl must bleed on her wedding night to prove she is a virgin;
- an intact hymen is a sign of virginity;
- FGM (female genital mutilation) is part of Islam;
- that a wife must never refuse her husband sex;
- tampons are haram;
- that your daughter's virginity is more important than your son's.

These are all incorrect and belief in these damaging ideas jeopardises healthy sexual relationships. The FaceBook page of the American Muslim Organization, Heart Women & Girls has an informative post on 'The Truth about Hymens'[65] and a 'A Story about Tampons.'[66]

WHAT CAN YOU DO TO HELP YOUR TEEN?

Remind your teen that there are seven people whom Allah will shade on the Day of Judgment.

One of them is a youth who grows up worshipping Allah, because adolescence is the most challenging age in terms of temptation and peer pressure. Remaining chaste is an honorable value in the sight of Allah. Remind them of being blessed with a GREAT REWARD should they resist temptation. They are honoring their dignity as stated in the Qur'an surah 17, verse 70 'And surely we have honored the children of Adam.' We are here to please Allah, not other people.

Reassure your child that not everyone is having sex.

There are fewer teens having sex than your children are led to believe. Research always confirms this discrepancy in the numbers. A 2013 British Columbia, Canada study of 30,000 Grade 7-12s found 39% of 17-year-olds had engaged in intercourse.[67] A more recent 2017 analysis by the New York Times found that 42% of 15- to 19-year-olds say they've had sex at least once by the age of 19.[68] Though these numbers are high, the majority of teens are not having sex. A 2019 study[69] in the Journal of School Health found that teens who don't date are more socially adept, happier and less depressed. They also received higher ratings for leadership skills from their teachers.

Discuss their naturally increasing desire with your teen.

A conversation about this should include something like: 'Being young and single while dealing with hormones and emotions is not easy. All you see, read and watch are images of love, romance, passion, and sex, and you want to experience that closeness to someone, which is normal. Allah has awakened our thoughts and desires in these years. You may have friends that are dating, and you are going to feel like you are missing out. The peer pressure will be hard. You are going to hear: "Sex is fun," "What's wrong with you?" "How will you know if you're sexually compatible?" "It's your body," "Are you a prude?" "Have you got hang-ups?" "You're old-fashioned," and "Everybody does it," among many others. You have your whole life ahead of you for marriage and sex. Give yourself something to look forward to. Sure, you may be missing out now, but that is temporary enjoyment. Abstaining now is choosing short-term pain for a long-term gain. You may hear people say, "How do you know you are sexually compatible?" When you get married, you will create sexual compatibility in your efforts to please each other; you don't need to have tried out different people. The love you will experience in a marriage will be very different from the infatuation/love you will experience while dating.

Temptation is all around us. Even Prophet Yusuf was presented with temptation and had to guard his chastity. "And she, in whose house he was, sought to seduce him from his (true) self: She fastened the doors, and said, 'Now come, thou (dear one)!' He said, 'God forbid!" (Qur'an 12:23).

You can decide to stay away from dating right from the start, so you don't have to suffer the pain and heartbreak of a short relationship. If you make that choice, you also don't have to be in a position of having to repent. It is going to take patience and strength to go through this. Allah knows what is best for us, and there is a reason why dating isn't allowed. Your soul is being protected. Make du'a and ask Allah to help you in this struggle.

I can't tell you what to do. That now is between you and Allah because you are accountable for your actions and the Qur'an tells us "And everyone of them Will come to Him singly On the Day of Judgement" (19:95).'

There is no compulsion in religion. We cannot make our children choose abstinence. We can only guide and empower them to come to that decision themselves and continue to make du'a that they do make the right choice. Healthy conversations around sex and sexuality increase the chances of them choosing to delay sex.

If you find out that your son or daughter has a boyfriend or girlfriend, the YouTube clip 'How Two Moms Dealt with Their Sons' Secret Girlfriends' by Hina Khan-Mukhtar is helpful in outlining how two different Muslim families dealt with this situation.[70]

Remind them of the best coping strategy

Over 1500 studies have found that those who are religious and pray have better physical and mental health, and greater well-being. They can cope with stress better, feel more hope and optimism, and experience less depression and anxiety.[71] The Qur'an tells us the same: '...Whosoever follows My guidance, will not lose his way, nor fall Into misery' (20:123).

WE'RE JUST FRIENDS

I played the YouTube clip 'Why Men and Women Can't be Friends' for a class of high schoolers, and then we discussed whether guys and girls could be friends. In the video, this question is posed to young adult guys and girls on campus. The girls answered yes to the question, while the guys responded with a no. Boys always found themselves developing an attraction to any girl that was a 'friend' to them.[72]

Let your child know that if their emotions are taking hold of them, they should step back and ask, 'Am I ok with where this is heading?' If you are in a situation which is going to lead to a relationship, avoid situations where you are alone. Keep to meeting in larger groups.

PETTING

I talked about petting at this point. 'While you are getting to know someone, the temptation is there anytime you are alone with them, especially as the attraction grows. Allah created us to have sexual desire. You may be at a stage where you hold hands and hug each other. Then, the kissing starts and before you know it a quick kiss becomes more intense kissing. Now you will want to start touching each other on top of your clothes, which can quickly move to touching under your clothes. It will be hard to make the right choice because it is going to feel exciting and good. Being sexually attracted to someone does not mean you are in love with them; this is generally lust. You are too young to decide you want to marry this person. The person you are now, and the person you want in your life as you get older, are going to change. You are in a situation right now where you might not make the right decision.'

HALAL DATING

Teens have asked me if there is such a thing as halal dating. They think that as long as intercourse is avoided, it's all good. I replied that 'It can be easy to convince yourself that it's okay to be dating someone who is also Muslim because you may end up getting married, so you have only had sexual relations with your future spouse. You may have once had the intention of possibly marrying this person, but then you break up. Once you start down the road of having a relationship with someone and having sex with them, it becomes much easier to do it again, which takes you further away from Allah.

Get to know someone before marriage, but in Islam, you need to do it without sex. Your judgment isn't going to be clouded because you are not in a physical relationship. Have patience, and if love develops where you see a future with someone in shaa Allah, then get married.'

If you are dating...

Some high schoolers let me know that they were dating (without their parents' knowledge) and some also were sexually active. It was good for those students to hear the message above, but they needed to also be aware that there was a way back, so I did bring up tawbah or repentance. I knew this was relevant and important because a student wrote on an anonymous note that she had sex but now felt terrible about it. I stated that 'We are human beings, so that makes us imperfect and we make mistakes. Allah wants us to repent by leaving the sin. He wants to forgive you so you can't keep engaging in sex and think you can keep repenting.

Chapter 39, verses 53-54 of the Qur'an say "O my Servants who have transgressed against their souls! Despair not of the Mercy of God: for God forgives All sins: for He is Oft-Forgiving, Most Merciful. Turn ye to your Lord (in repentance) and bow to His (Will), before The Penalty comes on you: After that ye shall not Be helped." When Allah decreed the creation, He wrote in His Book which is with Him on His throne: My mercy prevails over My wrath (Sahih Bukhari: 3022).'

I also didn't want those who weren't ready to repent to feel judged. I stated, 'It is not my place to judge anyone's choice or tell them what to do. If you are in a relationship that you want to continue in, that is your choice to own. You both have the same sexual rights and responsibilities, so I want you to think about two things:

Firstly, if you are going to become sexually active or already are, make sure it is a decision that you both are happy with. Take precautions to keep yourself safe and healthy. Protect yourself from STIs and pregnancy. Find out about contraception, including emergency contraception. The Alberta sexual education school curriculum site (www.teachingsexualhealth.ca) has regularly updated information about the different types of contraception. There is a Birth Control Centre here in Edmonton which offers confidential advice to teens to help you.' I also handed out information on available resources.

'Secondly, make sure this relationship is a healthy one. It should be free of physical, emotional, and sexual abuse. Physical violence uses or threatens to use force like hitting, punching, kicking, and so on. Emotional violence uses words or actions to control, humiliate, or degrade you. This is someone always wanting to know where you are, checking your phone, and taking you away from your friends and family. Don't mistake controlling behavior for love. Sexual violence is forcing someone to engage in any sexual activity without their consent. Prophet Muhammad (PBUH) is our role model. He was a caring and loving husband who NEVER hit a woman. Do not accept any disrespect or abuse.'

Teens must learn about the difference between love and infatuation and what a healthy relationship looks like, and this was the next area of discussion. These are the conversations I had with teens. Your conversation may look different, but I hope you can take away something from my conversations with youths and teens and incorporate them into your own.

LOVE VERSUS INFATUATION

'Infatuation often occurs at the start of a relationship based on physical and sexual chemistry. You feel intense emotions towards someone at this stage. This is different from love. People will show their best side, not their more difficult side, and infatuation can easily cause you to enter a relationship quickly, which is never a good idea. This can cause a person to become obsessive and possessive of the other person, and one or both may feel pressured to stay in the relationship. Love takes time and honors each person. Love enriches the lives of the two people it touches. It makes people feel safe, loved, and respected in that relationship. It requires commitment, and that is why marriage is important in Islam. Marriage is giving you your right to a sexually fulfilling relationship.'

Teens need to understand the qualities that make up a healthy relationship so that one day, when they are ready for marriage or if they choose to enter a relationship before marriage, they will pick someone worthy. This knowledge will also help them to recognize abuse should they find themselves in an unhealthy relationship.

WHAT IS A HEALTHY RELATIONSHIP?

Sexual assault is most common in the age group of 15- to 24-years-old, so it is vital for teens to understand consent and be knowledgeable about the differences between healthy and unhealthy relationships.

A healthy relationship has the following qualities: equality, respect, good communication, safety, empathy, trust, independence, support, and the ability to resolve conflict.[73]

These qualities of a healthy relationship should be discussed with your child. Ask them, 'What kind of a husband/wife do you want to have? What qualities do you want them to have? What behaviour would demonstrate that?' Teens must lead the discussion about how these qualities would look in a relationship. The main message needs to be that you should always feel like you can be yourself and feel safe and respected.

I shared the fact that 'The Dalai Lama once said you should marry someone you love to talk to. Looks will fade, and you are going to need good conversation to carry you through the years.'

Islamic views on a 'Healthy Relationship'

The following verses in the Qur'an clearly outline what a marital relationship entails. The traits and emotions include love, peace, tranquility, joy, support, mercy, kindness, honor, equity, protection, and mutual consultation. These were shared with the high schoolers.

- 'And among His signs is this, that He created for you mates from among Yourselves, that ye may dwell in peace and tranquillity with them, And He has put love and mercy between your (hearts): Verily in that are signs for those who reflect' (30:21).

- It is He Who created you from a single person, and made his mate of like nature, in order that he might dwell with her in love' (7:189).

- '...Grant unto us wives and offspring who will be the comfort of our eyes...' (25:74).

- '...live with them on a footing of kindness and equity' (4:19).

- '...who (conduct) their affairs by mutual consultation...' (42:38).

- 'They are your garments and ye are their garments' (2:187).

- '...Nor defame nor be sarcastic to each other, nor call each other by (offensive) nicknames...' (49:11).

- 'Men are the protectors and maintainers of women because God has given the one more (strength) than the other, and because they support them from their means' (4:34).

There are also Hadiths which provide commentary on relationships like:

'The Muslim is he from whose tongue and hand a Muslim is safe' (Sahih Al-Bukhari 11, Book 2, Hadith 4) and 'The best of you is the one who is best to his wife' (Sahih Ibn Hibban; Al Ihsan, Hadith: 4786, 4977).

In my talk with the high schoolers, we also discussed consent and the idea that 'Permission must be given to engage in any sexual activity. Both verbal and non-verbal communication must be in agreement and saying yes. Sex without consent is sexual assault. You should never feel pressured to say yes or scared to say no during sexual activity. You set your boundaries. You can withdraw consent and change your mind at any time. You have to consent every single time you have sex. You must be informed, comfortable and willing to engage in sexual activity.'

Since the first *Fifty Shades of Grey* movie was out, Muslim teens asked about BDSM (bondage, discipline, submission, and masochism). I explained that 'Some people like to have their sexual experiences coupled with pain where they either give or receive pain. This isn't behavior Muslims should engage in because sex is an expression of love, not pain.'

A few questions that came up when I did a workshop with young people over the age of 16 were:

How do you know when you are in love?

I offered this response: 'We are born to be connected to others. Falling in love is the ultimate connection. You will miss the person when you don't see them. You enjoy their company and genuinely like them. You also want your family and friends to like them. Conversation flows easily, and you feel like you can be yourself. You feel connected and want to see them grow and succeed. You might feel butterflies or have warm feelings for them when they walk into the room.'

What are some Deal-breakers when searching for a Marriage Partner?

'We all have different deal-breakers. We are human and might have preferences in terms of someone's cultural background because of a feeling of familiarity and therefore comfort. It is perfectly normal to want to feel physically attracted to someone. Everyone will have their own list of criteria that are important in a partner, whether it's a sense of humor, spontaneous nature, liking to engage in political discussions, and so on, but you should never compromise on respect, compassion, and humility. It's better if you both practice Islam at similar levels. Don't pick someone in the hopes of changing them. People can change in some ways, but by the time they are old enough to marry, their inherent character is formed.'

Parents, please be reasonable in your expectations of a spouse for your children. They don't have to be marrying someone from the same tribe or village, who speaks the same dialect. They also don't have to marry only university-educated partners. It is more about the compatibility of mind and soul than it is about educational levels. Boys shouldn't feel the pressure to have a certain income or type of house to get married. All of this contributes to children going down the road of zina. Make it easy for them to get married young. Remember that the priority for marriage should be piety, according to Prophet Muhammad (PBUH).

In summary, the key points to remember about talking to your children about sex are:

- Start when they are young

- Remove stigma

- No shaming

- Be honest

- Become an askable adult

- Look out for teachable moments

- Talk and listen

- Islam is sex-positive and sex is a gift from Allah

- Talk about anatomy, puberty, menstruation, wet dreams, masturbation, intercourse and PLEASE talk about pornography
- Remind them that pornography wants to pull them in but it will ruin their ability to have a real healthy and loving relationship

- Keep the message positive—No dating and pre-marital sex because Allah wants to protect you and knows what is best for you

- Model a healthy relationship

- Monitor technology—No computers/TV in bedroom, watch what they are watching, use parental controls, check smartphones, learn about apps

- Remind them that Allah is watching and wants to reward them

- Remind your teen that there are seven people whom Allah will shade on the Day of Judgment

- Reassure your child that not everyone is having sex

- Discuss their naturally increasing desire

- Talk about healthy relationships and marriage

- Remind them to make du'a to resist temptation and to meet a righteous spouse. Encourage them to be regular with prayers. I used to tell my sons 'Take care of your prayers and your prayers will take care of you.'

CONCLUSION

Children are entering puberty at earlier ages now. Our children are growing up with smartphones. They have access to social media and the internet and both the good and the bad that these can offer. Our role is to keep them safe and healthy while navigating this digital world. Letting our children get sex-ed from peers or online is exposing them to potentially incorrect information and unhealthy views of sexual relationships which can be detrimental to their well-being.

According to research, 50% of parents found beginning conversations with their children about sex to be uncomfortable, while more than 40% only had those discussions after their children became sexually active.[74] It's okay to be uncomfortable at the thought of these conversations but don't be one of the 40% because you left it too late.

You can only help your child achieve their full potential through your connection and communication with them. Parents, you hold a lot of influence; you must put it to use. The end goal for our children is not just to tell them what not to do or tell them about the mechanics of sex. Our end goal is to teach them how to build a healthy relationship and make them see sex as a blessing from Allah that nurtures the bond of that relationship.

We want our children to resist the pressure to be sexually active and to have a healthy and sexually fulfilling relationship within the confines of a marriage one day. If we start with a good mindset and active involvement when they are young, it will help them get there when they are older, in shaa Allah. Raising God-conscious, compassionate children into adults who make a positive influence on the world and who will make du'a for you is your legacy.

We cannot legislate abstinence. We can only build the foundation of faith and hope our children make the right choices.

These topics are essential to cover with our children because we must respond to the changing times. Talking about sex and sexuality will protect them and empower them to make good choices. I hope you feel more confident and inspired to start these conversations, even if having them is out of your comfort zone. It's okay to be uncomfortable but you can do it. Keep the information coming often, and in little chunks, so that the messages are reinforced. All this information can be framed within an

Islamic perspective. Sex has come from Allah for procreation and pleasure. We have to remind ourselves that sex is a good and loving thing, and sexual desire normal so we need to become more comfortable talking about it.

Islam is also a religion of hope. Keep making du'a for your children and keep asking Allah for help in parenting. Ask for patience and understanding in dealing with them. Ask Allah to guide and keep your children on the straight path. Also, be kind to yourself. Despite our best intentions, sometimes our children will reject Islam or go astray. If you have done your best, the outcome is out of your control. This does not mean you have failed as a parent. Everyone has free will, and there is no compulsion in religion. When parents raise children in a healthy Islamic environment, the chances are high that those children will return to their values one day.

Yes, the world has spiraled into a place that doesn't honor God. I have heard junior high kids declare their atheism. Have hope and faith in your children and let them feel it. There are plenty of children and teens that grow up and hold onto the rope of Allah and maintain their values. In the past, I worked for over a year with a fantastic group of 16- to 24-year-olds that were dynamic, confident, proud, and practicing Muslims. Many Muslim youths are doing amazing things to show a positive side to Islam, and plenty of teens are donning the hijab by choice.

Do not lose hope, parents. Just remember that the time that the Prophet lived in was challenging. Sexual promiscuity abounded, but he didn't despair. Have confidence that you have the knowledge to speak to your child and put this knowledge into practice. This is a necessary step to raise confident and practicing Muslim children who can make the right decisions when it comes to sex. May Allah make it easy for them to find righteous spouses. May Allah make it easy for you to parent and guide your children on the right path.

Remember, Prophet Muhammad (PBUH) said, 'Whoever guides someone to goodness will have a similar reward.'

REFERENCES

1. Mohajir, N. (2016). The Serious Implications for Denying Muslim Youth Sex Education. [online]. Available at: http://heartwomenandgirlsorg/2016/01/14/the-serious-implications-for-denying-muslim-youth-sex-education/

2. Let the Quran speak. (July 11, 2015). Sex Ed: An Islamic Perspective Farrah Marfatia. Retrieved from https://www.youtube.com/watch?v=437drjZwQaw&fbclid=IwAR3EbRyV-J34e6MGG3wY1Mz0mr54vfC0mzTmx_zrc-k_dM3nbbut9H7-4U1Y

3. NSPCC (2016). Age Verification in the Digital Economy Bill Public Bill Committee Evidence from the NSPCC [online]. Available at: https://publications.parliament.uk/pa/cm201617/cmpublic/digitaleconomy/memo/DEB44.pdf

4. Boonstra. (2010). Sex Education: Another Big Step Forward - And a Step Back. The Guttmacher Policy Review, 13(2), 27-28.

5. Centers for Disease Control and Prevention. (2011). Parent and guardian resources. [online]. Available at: http://www.cdc.gov/TeenPregnancy/Parents.htm

6. Ali-Faisal, Sobia F. (2014). Crossing sexual barriers: The influence of background factors and personal attitudes on sexual guilt and sexual anxiety among Canadian and American Muslim women and men. Electronic Theses and Dissertations. 5051. https://scholar.uwindsor.ca/etd/5051

7. Albert, B. (2012). With one voice: America's adults and teens sound off about teen pregnancy. Washington, DC: The National Campaign to Prevent Teen and Unplanned Pregnancy. [online]. Available at: https://success1st.org/uploads/3/4/5/1/34510348/wov_2012.pdf - PDFp.7

8. Ali-Faisal, Sobia F. (2014). Crossing sexual barriers: The influence of background factors and personal attitudes on sexual guilt and sexual anxiety among Canadian and American Muslim women and men. Electronic Theses and Dissertations. 5051.
https://scholar.uwindsor.ca/etd/5051

9. Mohajir, N. (2016). The Serious Implications for Denying Muslim Youth Sex Education. [online]. Available at:
http://heartwomenandgirlsorg/2016/01/14/the-serious-implications-for-denying-muslim-youth-sex-education/

10. Niamatullah, Abu Eesa. (2014, March 2). The latest guidance which was released concerning sex education in UK schools is shocking to say the least, especially as it has a good chance of being implemented after support from the Schools Minister. [FaceBook Status Update].Retrieved from:
https://www.facebook.com/pg/AbuEesaPersonal/posts/?ref=page_internal

11. Qadhi, Y. Raising Teenagers in a world of Pornography, Drugs & Pre-marital Sex. Oct 4, 2015. [online]. Available at:
https://www.youtube.com/watch?v=IBPvzU4gr2o

12. MacNamara, D. When Peers Matter More Than Parents. January 2015 [online]. Available at:
http://macnamara.ca/portfolio/when-peers-matter-more-than-parents/

13. Abbasi, J. Why 6-Year-Old Girls Want To Be Sexy. Published: 07/16/2012 [online].Available at:
https://www.huffpost.com/entry/6-year-old-girls-sexy_n_1679088

14. American Psychological Association, Task Force on the Sexualization of Girls. (2007). Report of the APA task force on the sexualization of girls. Washington, DC: American Psychological Association.Retrieved from
http://www.apa.org/pi/women/programs/girls/report.aspx.

15. Mignucci, M. Back to School Awards 2017: The Best Health and Wellness Products. June 1, 2017. [online]. Available at: https://www.teenvogue.com/gallery/back-to-school-awards-2017-health-wellness-products

16. Relaxnews. Too Much Screen Time Linked to Drop In Kids' Brain Functioning: Canadian Study. September 27, 2018. [online]. Available at: https://www.huffingtonpost.ca/2018/09/27/kids-screen-time-effects_a_23543754/

17. Teen Futures Media Network. Teen Health and the Media [online]. Available at: http://depts.washington.edu/thmedia/view.cgi?section=medialiteracy&page=fastfacts

18. PiperJaffary. Taking Stock with Teens Survey – Fall 2018 Results. October 22, 2018. [online]. Available at: https://piper2.bluematrix.com/sellside/EmailDocViewer?encrypt=3aac149e-6526-47aa-af46-f75b785e29cf&mime=pdf&co=Piper&id=kleswing@businessinsider.com&source=mail

19. Saraiya, S. Netflix and Pen15 Are Changing the Way TV Does Teen Sex. February 8, 2019. [online]. Available at: https://www.vanityfair.com/hollywood/2019/02/sex-education-big-mouth-pen15-teenage-sex-puberty-netflix

20. Ybarra, M. Is Sex in the Media Related to Sexual Behavior Among Teens? How do teens exposed to a lot versus a little sexual media differ? June 28, 2016. [online]. Available at: https://www.psychologytoday.com/ca/blog/connected/201606/is-sex-in-the-media-related-sexual-behavior-among-teens

21. Mignucci, M. '13 Reasons Why' Release Was Linked To An Increase in Suicides Among Teens, & Here's What You Should Know. Apr 30, 2019. [online]. Available at: https://www.bustle.com/p/13-reasons-why-release-was-linked-to-increase-in-suicides-among-teens-heres-what-you-should-know-17268559

22. Covenant Eyes. Pornography Statistics. [online]. Available at: https://www.covenanteyes.com/pornstats/#stats_title

23. Warner, R. and MacLaughlin, K. The Detrimental Effects of Pornography on Small Children. Dec 19, 2017. [online]. Available at: https://www.netnanny.com/blog/the-detrimental-effects-of-pornography-on-small-children/

24. Sax, L. Fortnite, Boys, and Self-Control. What can research tell us about the latest videogame craze? May 12, 2018. [online]. Available at: https://www.psychologytoday.com/us/blog/sax-sex/201805/fortnite-boys-and-self-control

25. Jackson, L.A, von Eye, A., Fitzgerald, H.E, Witt, E.A. and Zhao, Y. "Internet use, videogame playing and cell phone use as predictors of children's body mass index (BMI), body weight, academic performance, and social and overall self-esteem," Computers in Human Behaviour 27, no. 1 (2011):599-604,

26. Sax, L. Fortnite, Boys, and Self-Control. What can research tell us about the latest videogame craze? May 12, 2018. [online]. Available at: https://www.psychologytoday.com/us/blog/sax-sex/201805/fortnite-boys-and-self-control

27. Harding, N. Abuse in the Playground. Shocking rise of sexual abuse by primary school kids attacking their peers. 27 Jan 2019. [online]. Available at: https://www.thesun.co.uk/fabulous/8266620/rise-of-pre-teen-sexual-predators-in-uk-schools/

28. Warner, R. and MacLaughlin, K. The Detrimental Effects of Pornography on Small Children. Dec 19, 2017. [online]. Available at: https://www.netnanny.com/blog/the-detrimental-effects-of-pornography-on-small-children/

29. Howse, P. 'Pornography addiction worry' for tenth of 12 to 13-year-olds. 31 March 2015. [online]. Available at: https://www.bbc.com/news/education-32115162

30. Break Free From Sexually Addictive Behaviors For Good. Purify Your Gaze. [webpage].Retrieved from: www.Purifyyourgaze.com

31. About Islam. Purify Your Gaze: Muslims Healing from Porn Addiction Interview with Zeyad Ramadan, Founder of Purify Your Gaze Interview. March 2016. [online]. Available at: https://aboutislam.net/family-life/your-society/purify-gaze-muslims-healing-porn-addiction/

32. Awaad, R. and Mojaddidi, H. Parenting in the Age of Social Media. April 24, 2017. [online]. Available at: https://www.youtube.com/watch?v=Vov6uLZCjuU

33. and 34. Abu-Ras, W., Ahmed, S., Arfken, C. (2010). Alcohol use among U.S. Muslim college students: Risk and protective factors. Journal of Ethnicity in Substance Abuse, 9(3), p. 206-220.

35. Ahmed, S. & Ezzeddine, M. (2009). Challenges and Opportunities Facing American Muslim Youth, Journal of Muslim Mental Health, 4:2, 159-174, DOI: 10.1080/15564900903245782

36. Suleiman, O. Infographic – Internalized Islamophobia: Exploring the Faith and Identity Crisis of American Muslim Youth. May 14, 2017. [online]. Available at: https://yaqeeninstitute.org/omar-suleiman/infographic-internalized-islamophobia-exploring-the-faith-and-identity-crisis-of-american-muslim-youth/#.XcnOWzNKiUl

37. and 38. Ahmed, S. & Ezzeddine, M. (2009). Challenges and Opportunities Facing American Muslim Youth, Journal of Muslim Mental Health, 4:2, 159-4, DOI: 10.1080/15564900903245782

39. Seifert, S. Age-Appropriate Chores. [online]. Available at: https://www.focusonthefamily.com/parenting/parenting-challenges/motivating-kids-to-clean-up/age-appropriate-chores

40. Fishel, A. The most important thing you can do with your kids? Eat dinner with them. Jan 12, 2015. [online]. Available at: https://www.washingtonpost.com/posteverything/wp/2015/01/12/the-most-important-thing-you-can-do-with-your-kids-eat-dinner-with-them/

41. Dyck, D. Children as young as eight are voluntarily sharing nude photos online: RCMP, January 2, 2019. [online]. Available at: https://nationalpost.com/news/canada/children-as-young-as-8-are-voluntarily-sharing-nude-photos-police

42. Harding, N. Abuse in the Playground. Shocking rise of sexual abuse by primary school kids attacking their peers. 27 Jan 2019. [online]. Available at: https://www.thesun.co.uk/fabulous/8266620/rise-of-pre-teen-sexual-predators-in-uk-schools/

43. http://donate.islamicnetwork.net/youth?fbclid=IwAR0T9ZmVUrpdw7d4ocXG1z-nNwxa5n9WNptgLvoPsOJ94jJj5W7IeUAw-Ug

44. Gilkerson, L. & Gilkerson, T. [online]. https://www.intoxicatedonlife.com/having-the-talk-optin

45. Moghul,H. Muslim men don't know how to talk about love. But they need to. Feb 14, 2014 [online]. Available at: https://www.theguardian.com/commentisfree/2014/feb/14/salaam-love-muslim-men-relationships

46. Alberta Health Services. (2019). [online]. Available at: https://teachingsexualhealth.ca/parents/information-by-age/

47. NSPCC. [online]. Available at: https://www.nspcc.org.uk/preventing-abuse/keeping-children-safe/underwear-rule/

48. Manning, S. The book that dares to take on transgender myths told to children: Experts reveal psychologists are scared to question transgender idiology, GPs are afraid of being branded transphobic and teens are being wrongly diagnosed.13 July 2019. [online]. Available at: https://www.dailymail.co.uk/news/article-7244783/Academics-medical-experts-fears-children-number-seeking-sex-change-operations-sky-rockets.html

49. Life in the womb (9 months in 4 minutes) HD – Presented to You from PSNX. Jan 13, 2015. [online] Available at: https://www.youtube.com/watch?v=K7kaw40pPYw

50. Parveen, N. School defends LGBT lessons after religious parents complain. 31 Jan 2019. [online]. Available at: https://www.theguardian.com/education/2019/jan/31/school-defends-lgbt-lessons-after-religious-parents-complain

51. Ali-Faisal, S. Are Parents Getting in the way of Sex Education. December 11, 2015. [online]. Available at: http://heartwomenandgirls.org/2015/12/11/are-parents-getting-in-the-way-of-sex-education/

52. Ontario Ministry of Education (2019). The Ontario Curriculum: Elementary Health and Physical Education. [online]. Available at: http://www.edu.gov.on.ca/eng/curriculum/elementary/health.html

53. Mohajir, N. (2016). The Serious Implications for Denying Muslim Youth Sex Education. [online]. Available at: http://heartwomenandgirlsorg/2016/01/14/the-serious-implications-for-denying-muslim-youth-sex-education/

54. Long, J. Sex ed in Alberta is not just an LGBTQ issue. February 7, 2019. [online] Available at: https://nationalpost.com/pmn/news-pmn/sex-ed-in-alberta-is-not-just-an-lgbtq-issue

55. Ali-Faisal, S. Are Parents Getting in the way of Sex Education. Dec 11, 2015. [online]. Available at: http://heartwomenandgirls.org/2015/12/11/are-parents-getting-in-the-way-of-sex-education/

56. Alberta Ministry of Education. Human Sexuality Education. [online]. Available at: https://education.alberta.ca/media/160196/health.pdf (K-9) https://education.alberta.ca/media/160199/calm.pdf (10-12)

57. Fight the New Drug. How Many People Are On Porn Sites Right Now? (Hint: It's A Lot). September 3, 2019. [online]. Available at: https://fightthenewdrug.org/by-the-numbers-see-how-many-people-are-watching-porn-today/

58. Covenant Eyes. Pornography Statistics. [online]. Available at: https://www.covenanteyes.com/pornstats/#stats_title

59. Betkowski, B. "1 in 3 boys heavy porn users, study shows," Eurekalert.org, Feb. 23, 2007.
http://www. eurekalert.org/pub_releases/2007-02/uoa-oit022307.php

60. Johnson, L. Clinical psychologist warns of dangers of high porn usage. June 2, 2019. [online]. Available at: https://edmontonjournal.com/news/local-news/clinical-psychologist-warns-of-dangers-of-high-porn-usage

61. Reid, R. 52% of Young People Say They Don't Get The Sex Talk They Need At home Or At School. November 29, 2019. [online]. Available at: https://graziadaily.co.uk/life/real-life/sex-education-uk/

62. Davis, V. and Jenson, K. 7 Ways Predators and Porn will Target Kids in 2019 – Be Prepared Not Scared. January 8, 2019. [online]. Available at: https://www.protectyoungminds.org/2019/01/08/ways-predators-porn-target-kids-2019/

63. Miller, B. Largest Pornography Company Targets Video Game Industry. September 28, 2018. [online]. Available at: https://endsexualexploitation.org/articles/largest-pornography-company-targets-video-game-industry/

64. Greenfield, P.M. Inadvertent exposure to pornography on the Internet: Implications of peer-to-peer file-sharing networks for child development and families. Journal of Applied Developmental Psychology 25 (Nov/Dec 2004), p.741–750.

65. Heart Women & Girls. The Truth About Hymens. [FaceBook Status Update] Retrieved from: https://www.facebook.com/HEARTwomenandgirls/photos/pcb.10163395506785389/10163395503235389/?type=3&theater

66. Heart Women & Girls. A Story about Tampons. [FaceBook Status Update] Retrieved from: https://www.facebook.com/HEARTwomenandgirls/photos/pcb.10163372040600389/10163372034805389/?type=3&theater

67. Sexual & Reproductive Health – Alberta Health Services Calgary Zone. (2017). Youth sexuality: Stats and trends. Calgary: Author. [online]. Available at: https://tasccalberta.com/wp-content/uploads/2017/11/Youth-Sexuality-Trends-2017.pdf

68. Bakalar, N. Nearly Half of Teens Have had Sex by Age 19, Survey Finds. June 26, 2017. [online]. Available at: https://www.nytimes.com/2017/06/26/health/united-states-teenagers-sexual-activity.html

69. Douglas, B. & Orpinas, P. Social Misfit or Normal Development? Students Who Do Not Date. Journal of School Health, 2019; DOI: 10.1111/josh.12818

70. Muslim Community Center – MCC East Bay. How Two moms Dealt with Their Sons' Secret Girlfriends/ Hina Khan-Mukhtar. Oct 28, 2019. [online]. Available at: https://www.youtube.com/watch?v=nYFZJj3BcZk&fbclid=IwAR2vREx1wREezhoJ9wuXG5lMyT4Mzm2P8hcLcccYYYvNhOWmyyTXnVtZ-JU

71. Newsmax. Science Proves the Healing Power of Prayer, 31 March 2015. [online]. Available at: https://www.newsmax.com/Health/Headline/prayer-health-faith-medicine/2015/03/31/id/635623/

72. Why Men and Women Can't be Friends. [online]. Available at: https://www.youtube.com/watch?v=T_lh5fR4DMA

73. Canadian Red Cross. (2015). Healthy Youth Relationships Program Lessons for Youth-Serving Organizations. Ottawa.

74. Long, J. Sex ed in Alberta is not just an LGBTQ issue. February 7, 2019. [online] Available at: https://nationalpost.com/pmn/news-pmn/sex-ed-in-alberta-is-not-just-an-lgbtq-issue

USEFUL RESOURCES:

Pornography:

Good Pictures Bad Pictures Porn-Proofing Today's Young Kids by Kristen Jenson and illustrated by G. Poyner

https://www.protectyoungminds.org/resources/ - free resources (ebooks to download)
https://fightthenewdrug.org/

Raising Girls:

Girls on the edge: The Four Factors Driving the New Crisis for Girls by Leonard Sax

Raising Boys:

Boys adrift: The Five Factors Driving the Growing Epidemic of Unmotivated Boys and Underachieving Young Men by Leonard Sax

Parenting:

The collapse of parenting How We Hurt our Kids When We Treat Them Like Grown-Ups by Leonard Sax

Why Gender Matters: What parents and teachers need to know about the emerging science of sex differences (second edition) by Leonard Sax

Other parenting books I found helpful when my sons were young are:

Siblings without Rivalry by Adele Faber & Elaine Mazlish

How to talk so kids will listen; how to listen so kids will talk by Adele Faber & Elaine Mazlish

Kids are Worth It by Barbara Coloroso

Toxic Childhood by Sue Palmer

Loving your child is not enough by Nancy Samalin

Raising Resilient Children: Fostering Strength, Hope, and Optimism in Your Child by Robert Brooks and Sam Goldstein

Friend recommendations:

Peaceful Parent, Happy Siblings: How to Stop the Fighting and Raise Friends for Life by Dr. Laura Markham

Peaceful Parent, Happy Kids by Dr. Laura Markham

The Whole-Brain Child by Daniel J. Siegel and Tina Payne Bryson

No-drama Discipline by Daniel J. Siegel and Tina Payne Bryson

Sex Education – spiritually based

God's Design for Sex Series (4 book set) by Stan and Brenna Jones

Christian based parent booklet

https://www.covenanteyes.com/resources/parentbooklet/

https://www.intoxicatedonlife.com/category/parenting/sex-ed/

https://homeword.com/category/pornography/ (many useful categories to explore such as adolescence, sexuality, parenting, discipline etc.)

Conversation starters

https://www.mother.ly/child/35-engaging-questions-to-ask-instead-of-what-did-you-do-today

http://drkristiwolfe.com/conversation-starters/

Family tradition ideas

https://mommypotamus.com/family-tradition-ideas/

Apps and digital parenting

https://www.huffingtonpost.ca/entry/the-12-apps-that-every-parent-of-a-teen-should-know-about_n_56c34e49e4b0c3c55052a6ba?ri18n=true

https://wezift.com/parent-portal/blog/groupme-8-other-dangerous-apps-parents-should-know/

https://www.internetmatters.org/?utm_source=Facebook&utm_medium=social&utm_campaign=SocialSignIn

www.ingramcontent.com/pod-product-compliance
Lightning Source LLC
Chambersburg PA
CBHW030910080526
44589CB00010B/231